The Globalization

of War

The Globalization of War

America's "Long War"
against Humanity

Michel Chossudovsky

Global Research

About the author

Michel Chossudovsky is an award-winning author, Professor of Economics (emeritus) at the University of Ottawa, Founder and Director of the Centre for Research on Globalization (CRG), Montreal, Editor of Global Research. He has taught as visiting professor in Western Europe, Southeast Asia, the Pacific and Latin America. He has served as economic adviser to governments of developing countries and has acted as a consultant for several international organizations.

He is the author of eleven books including *The Globalization of Poverty and The New World Order* (2003), *America's "War on Terrorism"* (2005), *The Global Economic Crisis, The Great Depression of the Twenty-first Century* (2009) (Editor), *Towards a World War III Scenario: The Dangers of Nuclear War* (2011). He is a contributor to the Encyclopaedia Britannica. His writings have been published in more than twenty languages.

Michel Chossudovsky is a member of the Kuala Lumpur War Crimes Commission (KLWCC) which initiated the indictment against George W. Bush et al *"for crimes of torture and war crimes"*. (Judgement of the Kuala Lumpur War Crimes Tribunal (KLWCT), 11 May 2012) and on *"crimes of genocide"* against the State of Israel, (Judgement of the Tribunal, November 25, 2013).

In 2014, Michel Chossudovsky was awarded the Gold Medal for Merit of the Republic of Serbia for his writings on NATO's war on Yugoslavia.

The Globalization of War

America's "Long War" against Humanity

by Michel Chossudovsky

Global Research Publishers is a division of the Centre for Research on Globalization (CRG),

P.O. Box 55019, 11, rue Notre-Dame Ouest, Montréal, Québec, H2Y 4A7, Canada.

For more information, contact the publisher at the above address or by email at our website at www.globalresearch.ca.

FIRST EDITION

Cover Photo © Stocktrek Images/Getty Images

Cover graphics by Alexander Vlaanderen © Global Research, 2015

Page layout and book design by Réjean McKinnon

Printed and Bound in Canada

Printed on chlorine free 100% post-consumer recycled Canadian paper

ISBN 978-0-9737147-6-0

Library and Archives Canada cataloguing in publication

Chossudovsky, Michel

The Globalization of War: America's "Long war" against Humanity / by Michel Chossudovsky.

ISBN 978-0-9737147-6-0

1. United States--Foreign relations. 2. United States--Military policy. 3. North Atlantic Treaty Organization--Foreign relations. 4. North Atlantic Treaty Organization--Military policy. 5. Globalization. I. Title.

JZ1480.C46 2015   327.1'170973   C2014-907701-7
                                       C2014-900772-5

This book is dedicated

To the Hon. Rep. Lee Seok-ki for his commitment to political and civil rights in the Republic of Korea and his lifelong battle against the ROK's infamous National Security Law.

To my lifelong friend and mentor Professor Jules Dufour whose detailed geographical analysis of U.S. military bases reveals the true meaning of America's Worldwide hegemonic project.

Titles by Global Research Publishers

Michel Chossudovsky, *Towards a World War III Scenario, The Danger of Nuclear War,* 2012.

Michel Chossudovsky and Andrew Gavin Marshall (Editors), *The Global Economic Crisis, The Great Depression of the XXI Century,* 2010.

F. William Engdahl, *Seeds of Destruction: The Hidden Agenda of Genetic Manipulation,* 2007.

Michel Chossudovsky, *America's "War on Terrorism",* 2005.

Michel Chossudovsky, *The Globalization of Poverty and the New World Order,* 2003.

———— TABLE OF CONTENTS ————

PREFACE

The "globalization of war" is a hegemonic project. Major military and covert intelligence operations are being undertaken simultaneously in the Middle East, Eastern Europe, sub-Saharan Africa, Central Asia and the Far East. The U.S. military agenda combines both major theater operations as well as covert actions geared towards destabilizing sovereign states.

Under a global military agenda, the actions undertaken by the Western military alliance (U.S.-NATO-Israel) in Afghanistan, Pakistan, Palestine, Ukraine, Syria and Iraq are coordinated at the highest levels of the military hierarchy. We are not dealing with piecemeal military and intelligence operations. The July-August 2014 attack on Gaza by Israeli forces was undertaken in close consultation with the United States and NATO. The actions in Ukraine and their timing coincided with the onslaught of the attack on Gaza.

In turn, military undertakings are closely coordinated with a process of economic warfare which consists not only in imposing sanctions on sovereign countries but also in deliberate acts of destabilization of financial and currencies markets, with a view to undermining the enemies' national economies.

The United States and its allies have launched a military adventure which threatens the future of humanity. As we go to press, U.S. and NATO forces have been deployed in Eastern Europe including Ukraine. U.S. military intervention under a humanitarian mandate is proceeding in sub-Saharan Africa. The U.S. and its allies are threatening China under President Obama's "Pivot to Asia".

In turn, military maneuvers are being conducted at Russia's doorstep which could potentially lead to escalation.

The U.S. airstrikes initiated in September 2014 directed against Iraq and Syria under the pretext of going after the Islamic State are part of a scenario of military escalation extending from North Africa and the Eastern Mediterranean to Central and South Asia.

The Western military alliance is in an advanced state of readiness. And so is Russia.

Russia is heralded as the "Aggressor". U.S.-NATO military confrontation with Russia is contemplated.

Enabling legislation in the U.S. Senate under "The Russian Aggression Prevention Act" (RAPA) has "set the U.S. on a path towards direct military conflict with Russia in Ukraine."

> Any U.S.-Russian war is likely to quickly escalate into a nuclear war, since neither the U.S. nor Russia would be willing to admit defeat, both have many thousands of nuclear weapons ready for instant use, and both rely upon Counterforce military doctrine that tasks their military, in the event of war, to pre-emptively destroy the nuclear forces of the enemy.[1]

The Russian Aggression Prevention Act (RAPA) is the culmination of more than twenty years of U.S.-NATO war preparations, which consist in the military encirclement of both Russia and China:

> From the moment the Soviet Union collapsed in 1991, *the United States has relentlessly pursued a strategy of encircling Russia,* just as it has with other perceived enemies like China and Iran. *It has brought 12 countries in central Europe, all of them formerly allied with Moscow, into the NATO alliance. U.S. military power is now directly on Russia's borders.*[2]

Worldwide Militarization

From the outset of the post World War II period to the present, America's s global military design has been one of world conquest. War and globalization are intricately related. Militarization supports powerful economic interests. America's "Long War" is geared towards worldwide corporate expansion and the conquest of new economic frontiers.

The concept of the "Long War" is an integral part of U.S. military doctrine. Its ideological underpinnings are intended to camouflage the hegemonic project of World conquest. Its implementation relies on a global alliance of 28 NATO member states. In turn, the U.S. as well as NATO have established beyond the "Atlantic Region" a network of bilateral military alliances with "partner" countries directed against Russia, China, Iran and North Korea. What we are dealing with is a formidable military force, deployed in all major regions of the World. The "Long War" is based on the concept of "Self-Defense". The United States and the Western World are threatened. "The Long War" constitutes "an epic struggle against adversaries bent on forming a unified Islamic world to supplant western dominance". Underlying the "Long War", according to a study by the Rand Corporation, the Western World must address "three potential threats":

- those related to the ideologies espoused by key adversaries in the conflict,
- those related to the use of terrorism
- those related to governance (i.e., its absence or presence, its quality, and the predisposition of specific governing bodies to the United States and its interests).

... in order to ensure that this long war follows a favorable course, the United States will need to make a concerted effort across all three domains.[3]

Our objective in this book is to focus on various dimensions of America's hegemonic wars, by providing both a historical overview as well as an understanding of America's contemporary wars all of which, from a strategic viewpoint, are integrated.

Our analysis will focus on the dangers of nuclear war and the evolution of military doctrine in the post-9/11 era.

The central role of media propaganda as well as the failures of the anti-war movement will also be addressed. While the first chapter provides an overview, the subsequent chapters provide an insight into different dimensions of America's long war.

Chapter I, Imperial Conquest: America's "Long War" against Humanity provides a post World War II historical overview of America's wars from Korea and Vietnam to Afghanistan, Iraq and Syria. There is a continuum in U.S. Foreign Policy from the Truman Doctrine of the late 1940s to the neocons and neoliberals of the George W. Bush and Barack Obama administrations.

Part II focuses on the dangers of nuclear war and global nuclear radiation.

Chapter II, The Dangers of Nuclear War Conversations with Fidel Castro consists of Conversations with Fidel Castro and the author pertaining to the future of humanity and the post-Cold War process of militarization. This exchange took place in Havana in October 2010.

Chapter III focuses on the doctrine of **Pre-emptive Nuclear and the Role of Israel** in triggering a first strike use of nuclear weapons against Iran.

Chapter IV, The Threat of Nuclear War, North Korea or the United States? focuses on the persistent U.S. threat (since 1953) of using nuclear weapons against North Korea while labeling North Korea a threat to global security.

Chapter V, Fukushima: A Nuclear War without a War. The Unspoken Crisis of Worldwide Nuclear Radiation examines the dangers of nuclear energy and its unspoken relationship to nuclear weapons. Nuclear energy is not a civilian economic activity. It is an appendage of the nuclear weapons industry which is controlled by the so-called defense contractors. The powerful corporate interests behind nuclear energy and nuclear weapons overlap.

Part III illustrates at a country level, the *modus operandi* of U.S. military and intelligence interventions, including regime change and the covert support of terrorist organizations. The country case studies (Yugoslavia, Haiti, Libya, Iraq, Syria, Palestine, Ukraine) illustrate how individual nation states are destabilized as a result of U.S.-NATO covert operations and "humanitarian wars." While the nature and circumstances of these countries are by no means similar, there is a common thread. The purpose is to provide a comparative understanding of country-level impacts of America's long war against humanity. In all the countries analyzed, the intent has been to destroy, destabilize and impoverish sovereign countries.

Chapter VI, NATO's War on Yugoslavia: Kosovo "Freedom Fighters" Financed by Organized Crime examines the role of the Kosovo Liberation Army (KLA) as an instrument of political destabilization. In Yugoslavia, the endgame of NATO's intervention was to carve up a prosperous and successful "socialist market economy" into seven proxy states. The political and economic breakup of Yugoslavia in the 1990s served as a "role model" for subsequent "humanitarian military endeavors."

Chapter VII, The U.S. led Coup d'Etat in Haiti against the government of Jean Bertrand Aristide was carried out in February 2004 with the support of Canada and France. In a bitter irony, the U.S. ambassador to Haiti James Foley, had previously played a central role as U.S. special envoy to Yugoslavia, channeling covert support to the Kosovo Liberation Army (KLA). In Haiti, his responsibilities included U.S. aid to the *Front pour la Libération et la reconstruction nationale (FLRN)* (National Liberation and Reconstruction Front) largely integrated by former Tonton Macoute death squads. Closely coordinated with the process of regime change and military intervention, the IMF-World Bank macroeconomic reforms played a crucial role in destroying the national and impoverishing the Haitian population.

Chapter VIII, "Operation Libya" and the Battle for Oil: Redrawing the Map of Africa reveals the hidden agenda behind NATO's 2011 humanitarian war on Libya, which consisted in acquiring control and ownership of Libya's extensive oil reserves, that is, almost twice those of the United States of America. U.S. Africa Command (AFRICOM) played a key role in the war on Libya in coordination with NATO.

Libya is the gateway to the Sahel and Central Africa. More generally, what is at stake is the redrawing of the map of Africa at the expense of France's historical spheres of influence in West and Central Africa, namely a process of neocolonial re-division.

Chapter IX, The War on Iraq and Syria. Terrorism with a "Human Face": The History of America's Death Squads examines U.S.-NATO's covert war on Syria, which consists in creating Al Qaeda affiliated terrorist entities. The U.S.-led covert war consists in recruiting, training and financing Islamist death squads which are used as the foot-soldiers of the Western military alliance. The ultimate military objective is the destruction of both Iraq and Syria.

Chapter X, War and Natural Gas. The Israel Invasion and Gaza's Offshore Gas Fields focuses on Israel's attack directed against Gaza with a view to confiscating Gaza's offshore gas reserves.

In **Chapter XI, The U.S. has Installed a Neo-Nazi Government in Ukraine,** the structure of the U.S.-EU sponsored proxy regime in Kiev is examined. Key positions in government and the Armed Forces are in the hands of the two neo-Nazi parties. The Ukraine National Guard financed and trained by the West is largely integrated by Neo-Nazis Brown Shirts.

Part IV is entitled **Breaking the American Inquisition. Reversing the Tide of War** focuses on some of the contradictions of the antiwar movement. **Chapter XII, The "American Inquisition" and the "Global War on Terrorism"** analyzes the central role of America's "war on terrorism" doctrine in harnessing public support for a global war of conquest. The "Global War on Terrorism" (GWOT) is a fabrication based on the illusion that one man, Osama bin Laden, outwitted the multi-billion dollar U.S. intelligence community.

Today's "Global War on Terrorism" (GWOT) is a modern form of inquisition. It has all the essential ingredients of the French and Spanish Inquisitions. Going after "Islamic terrorists", carrying out a worldwide pre-emptive war to "protect the Homeland" are used to justify a military agenda.

In turn, "The Global War on Terrorism" is presented as a "Clash of Civilizations", a war between competing values and religions, when in reality it is an outright war of conquest, guided by strategic and economic objectives.

Chapter XII, "Manufactured Dissent", Colored Revolutions and the Antiwar Movement in Crisis examines the role of corporate foundations in funding dissent and the inability of "progressive" civil society organizations and antiwar collectives to effectively confront the tide of media disinformation and war propaganda.[4]

Michel Chossudovsky, Montreal, December 2014

Notes

1. See Steven Starr, "The Russian Aggression Prevention Act" (RAPA): A Direct Path to Nuclear War with Russia, Global Research, August 22, 2014.

2 Steven Kinzer, U.S. a full partner in Ukraine debacle, Boston Globe, March 3, 2014, emphasis added.

3 Christopher G. Pernin, Brian Nichiporuk, Dale Stahl, Justin Beck, Ricky Radaelli-Sanchez, Unfolding the Future of the Long War, Motivations, Prospects, and Implications for the U.S. Army, Rand Corporation, 2008.

4. The chapters in this book are based on research conducted over a period of more than ten years.

Acknowledgments

Research for this book was conducted over a fifteen year period extending from the 1999 NATO war against Yugoslavia to the present.

I am much indebted to Alex Vlaanderen, Julie Lévesque and Mahdi Darius Nazemroaya of the Centre for Research on Globalization (CRG) for their support in the editing process and the creative front cover graphics. I also extend my thanks and appreciation to Réjean McKinnon, for the careful typesetting, layout and production of the book and to Barbara Rudnicka for her invaluable assistance in the copyediting of the manuscript.

PART I

HISTORICAL OVERVIEW

Chapter I

Imperial Conquest: America's "Long War" against Humanity

Introduction

The U.S. and its NATO allies have embarked on a military adventure, "a long war", which threatens the future of humanity. This "war without borders" is intimately related to a worldwide process of economic restructuring, which has been conducive to the collapse of national economies and the impoverishment of large sectors of the World population.The U.S. weapons producers are the recipients of U.S. Department of Defense multibillion dollar procurement contracts for advanced weapons systems. In turn, "The Battle for Oil" in the Middle East and Central Asia directly serves the interests of the Anglo-American oil giants. The U.S. and its allies are "Beating the Drums of War" at the height of a worldwide economic depression.

The military deployment of U.S.-NATO forces coupled with "non-conventional warfare" –including covert intelligence operations, economic sanctions and the thrust of "regime change"– is occurring simultaneously in several regions of the world.

Central to an understanding of war, is the media campaign which grants it legitimacy in the eyes of public opinion. War has been provided with a humanitarian mandate under NATO's "Responsibility to Protect" (R2P). The victims of U.S. led wars are presented as the perpetrators of war. Civilians in Yugoslavia, Palestine, Ukraine, Libya, Syria and Iraq are responsible for their own deaths.

Meanwhile, the Commander in Chief of the largest military force on planet earth is presented as a global peace-maker. The granting of the Nobel "peace prize" in 2009 to President Barack Obama has become an integral part of the Pentagon's propaganda machine. It provides a human face to the invaders, it demonizes those who oppose U.S. military intervention.

The Nobel Committee says that President Obama has given the world "hope for a better future". The prize is awarded for Obama's "extraordinary efforts to strengthen international diplomacy and co-operation between peoples. The Committee has attached special importance to *Obama's vision of and work for a world without nuclear weapons.*"

> His diplomacy is founded in the concept that those who are to lead the world must do so on the basis of values and attitudes that are shared by the majority of the world's population.[1]

Realities are turned upside down. "War is Peace" said George Orwell. The media in chorus upholds war as a humanitarian endeavor. "Wars make us safer and richer" says the Washington Post.

The Big Lie becomes The Truth. In turn, upholding The Truth – through careful documentation and investigative analysis of the horrors of U.S. led wars– is casually categorized as "conspiracy theory".

While Washington wages a "Global War on Terrorism" (GWOT), those who forcefully oppose America's wars of aggression are branded as terrorists. War becomes peace, a worthwhile "humanitarian undertaking". Peaceful dissent becomes heresy.

With unfolding events in Ukraine and the Middle East, humanity is at a dangerous crossroads. At no time since the Cuban Missile Crisis has the World been closer to the unthinkable: a World War III scenario, a global military conflict involving the use of nuclear weapons.

The killing machine is deployed at a global level, within the framework of the unified combat command structure. It is routinely upheld by the institutions of government, the corporate media and the mandarins and intellectuals of The New World Order in Washington's think tanks and strategic studies research institutes, as an unquestioned instrument of peace and global prosperity.

A culture of killing and violence has become imbedded in human consciousness.

War is broadly accepted as part of a societal process: The Homeland needs to be "defended" and protected.

"Legitimized violence" and extrajudicial killings directed against "terrorists" are upheld in western democracies as necessary instruments of national security. A "humanitarian war" is upheld by the so-called international community. It is not condemned as a criminal act. Its main architects are rewarded for their contribution to world peace. Nuclear weapons are heralded by the U.S. government as instruments of peace. The pre-emptive use of nuclear weapons is categorized as an act of "self-defense" which contributes to an illusive concept of "global security". (See Chapter II).

The so-called "missile defense shield" or "Star Wars" initiative involving the first strike use of nuclear weapons has been developed globally in different regions of the world. The missile shield is largely directed against Russia, China, Iran and North Korea.

Meanwhile, in the context of unfolding events in Syria and Ukraine, there has been a breakdown of international diplomacy. Whereas a Neo-Nazi regime directly supported by the West has been installed in Kiev, the Russian Federation is now threatened by U.S.-NATO with military action on its Western frontier. (See Chapter IX).

New Cold War?

While this renewed East-West confrontation has mistakenly been labelled a "New Cold War", none of the safeguards of The Cold War era prevail. Russia has been excluded from the Group of Eight (G-8), which has reverted to the G-7 (Group of Seven Nations). Diplomacy has collapsed. There is no Cold War East-West dialogue between competing superpowers geared towards avoiding military confrontation. In turn, the United Nations Security Council has become a de facto mouthpiece of the U.S. State Department.

Moreover, nuclear weapons are no longer considered a "weapon of last resort" under The Cold War doctrine of "Mutual Assured Destruction" (MAD). Nuclear weapons are heralded by the Pentagon as "harmless to the surrounding civilian population because the explosion is underground". In 2002, the U.S. Senate gave the green light for the use of nuclear weapons in the conventional war theater. Nukes are part of the "military toolbox" to be used alongside conventional weapons.

The "Communist threat" of The Cold War era has been replaced by the worldwide threat of "Islamic terrorism". Whereas Russia and

China have become capitalist "free market" economies, a first strike pre-emptive nuclear attack against both countries is nonetheless contemplated.

China and Russia are no longer considered to be "a threat to capitalism". Quite the opposite. What is at stake is economic and financial rivalry between competing capitalist powers. The China-Russia alliance under the Shanghai Cooperation Organization (SCO) constitutes a "competing capitalist block" which undermines U.S. economic hegemony.

In Asia, the U.S. has contributed under its "Pivot to Asia" to encouraging its Asia-Pacific allies including Japan, Australia, South Korea, The Philippines and Vietnam to threaten and isolate China as part of a process of "military encirclement" of China, which gained impetus in the late 1990s.

Meanwhile, war propaganda has become increasingly pervasive. War is upheld as a peace-making operation.

When war becomes peace, the world is turned upside down. Conceptualization is no longer possible. An inquisitorial social system emerges. (See Chapter X). The consensus is to wage war. People can no longer think for themselves. They accept the authority and wisdom of the established social order.

An understanding of fundamental social and political events is replaced by a World of sheer fantasy, where "evil folks" are lurking. The objective of the "Global War on Terrorism" narrative –which has been fully endorsed by the U.S. administration– has been to galvanize public support for a worldwide campaign against heresy.

Global Warfare

The Pentagon's global military design is one of world conquest. The military deployment of U.S.-NATO forces is occurring in several regions of the world simultaneously.

The concept of the "Long War" has characterized U.S. military doctrine since the end of World War II. Worldwide militarization is part of a global economic agenda.

Militarization at the global level is instrumented through the U.S. military's Unified Command structure: the entire planet is divided up into geographic Combatant Commands under the control of the

Pentagon. U.S. Strategic Command (U.S.STRATCOM) Headquarters in Omaha, Nebraska plays a central role in coordinating military operations.

While surrounding and confronting Russia and China, new U.S. military bases have been set up with a view to establishing U.S. spheres of influence in every region of the World. There has been a reinforcement of the *six geographic commands* including the creation in 2008 of *United States Africa Command (AFRICOM)*.

As heralded by the Pentagon, AFRICOM becomes a "full-spectrum combatant command" responsible for what are described as "defense" and U.S. "national security" operations "through focused, sustained engagement with partners in support of our shared security objectives". AFRICOM's area of jurisdiction extends to the entire "African continent, its island nations, and surrounding waters".[2]

This U.S. militarization of Africa supports the concurrent economic conquest of the continent, the pillage of its natural resources, the acquisition of its extensive oil and gas reserves, etc.

AFRICOM is an instrument of a U.S. led neocolonial project in alliance with the United Kingdom which consists in expanding the Anglo-American sphere of influence specifically in Central Africa, Francophone West Africa and North Africa largely at the expense of France.

While the U.S. has military bases and/or facilities in more than 150 countries, with 160,000 active-duty personnel, the construction of new military bases is envisaged in Latin America including Colombia on the immediate border of Venezuela.

Military aid to Israel has increased. The Obama presidency has expressed its unbending support for Israel and the Israeli military, which is slated to play a key role in U.S.-NATO led wars in the Middle East. The unspoken agenda is the outright elimination of Palestine and the instatement of "Greater Israel".

"War without Borders"

The 2000 *Project for the New American Century (PNAC)*, first formulated by the Neocons, was predicated on "waging a war without borders". The PNAC is a neoconservative think tank linked to the Defense-Intelligence establishment, the Republican Party and the powerful Council on Foreign Relations (CFR) which plays a behind-the-scenes role in the formulation of U.S. foreign policy. In September 2000, a few months before the accession of George W. Bush to the White House, the Project for a New American Century (PNAC) published its blueprint for global domination under the title: "Rebuilding America's Defenses"[3] The PNAC's declared objectives are:

- defend the American homeland;
- *fight and decisively win multiple, simultaneous major theater wars;*
- *perform the "constabulary" duties* associated with shaping the security environment in critical regions;
- transform U.S. forces to exploit the "revolution in military affairs;"[4]

Former Deputy Defense Secretary Paul Wolfowitz, Defense Secretary Donald Rumsfeld and Vice President Dick Cheney (G. W. Bush administration) had commissioned the PNAC blueprint prior to the 2000 presidential elections.

The PNAC outlines a roadmap of military conquest. It calls for "the direct imposition of U.S. forward bases" throughout Central Asia and the Middle East "with a view to ensuring economic domination of the world, while strangling any potential "rival" or any viable alternative to America's vision of a "free market' economy".[5]

Distinct from theater wars, the so-called "constabulary functions" imply a form of global military policing using various instruments of military intervention including punitive bombings and the sending in of U.S. Special Forces, etc. Global constabulary functions also include covert operations and "regime change" all of which are carried out in accordance with a "humanitarian mandate".

Military actions are implemented simultaneously in different regions of the world (as outlined in the PNAC) as well as sequentially.

This military agenda undertaken under the banner of "Responsibility to Protect" largely prevails under the Obama presidency. Media propaganda has been instrumental in sustaining the fiction of humanitarian warfare.

New Weapons Systems

The PNAC's "revolution in military affairs" (meaning the development of new weapons systems) consists of *the Strategic Defense Initiative,* the concurrent weaponization of space and the development of a new generation of nuclear weapons.

The Strategic Defense Initiative, (Star Wars), not only includes the controversial "Missile Shield", but also a wide range of offensive laser-guided weapons with striking capabilities anywhere in the world, not to mention instruments of weather and climatic warfare under the High Frequency Active Auroral Research Program (HAARP). The latter is fully operational and has the ability of potentially triggering floods, droughts, hurricanes and earthquakes. From a military standpoint, HAARP is a weapon of mass destruction. Potentially, it constitutes an instrument of conquest capable of selectively destabilizing agricultural and ecological systems of entire regions.

Also contemplated is the Pentagon's so-called *FALCON program.* Formulated during the Bush Junior administration, FALCON is the ultimate New World Order weapons' system, to be used for global economic and political domination. It can strike from the continental U.S. anywhere in the World. It is described as a "global reach" weapon to be used to "react promptly and decisively to destabilizing or threatening actions by hostile countries and terrorist organizations".[5]

This hypersonic cruise weapon system developed by Northrop Grumman "would allow the U.S. to conduct effective, time-critical strike missions on a global basis without relying on overseas military bases."[6]

FALCON would allow the U.S. to strike, either in support of conventional forces engaged in a war theater or in punitive bombings directed against countries that do not comply with U.S. economic and political diktats.

The Military Road-map in the Middle East

According to (former) NATO Commander General Wesley Clark, the Pentagon's military road-map consists of a sequence of countries: "[The] Five-year campaign plan [includes]... a total of seven countries, beginning with Iraq, then Syria, Lebanon, Libya,

Iran, Somalia and Sudan." In *Winning Modern Wars* (page 130) General Clark states the following:

> "As I went back through the Pentagon in November 2001, one of the senior military staff officers had time for a chat. Yes, we were still on track for going against Iraq, he said. But there was more. This was being discussed as part of a five-year campaign plan, he said, and *there were a total of seven countries, beginning with Iraq, then Syria, Lebanon, Libya, Iran, Somalia and Sudan.*[6]

Syria and Iran

The ongoing war on Palestine, Syria and Iraq is a stepping stone towards a war on Iran, which could lead to a process of military escalation. Russia and China, which are allies of both Syria and Iran, are also targeted by U.S.-NATO. In Iraq, under the banner of a "civil war", an undercover war of aggression is being fought which essentially contributes to further destroying an entire country, its institutions, its economy. The undercover operation is part of an intelligence agenda, an engineered process which consists in transforming Iraq into an open territory.

Meanwhile, public opinion is led to believe that what is at stake is the confrontation between Shia and Sunni. America's military occupation of Iraq has been replaced by non-conventional forms of warfare. Realities are blurred. In a bitter irony, the aggressor nation is portrayed as coming to the rescue of a "sovereign Iraq".

The break up of Iraq and Syria along sectarian lines is a long-standing policy of the U.S. and its allies. The proposed re-division of both Iraq and Syria is broadly modeled on that of the Federation of Yugoslavia which was split up into seven "independent states" (Serbia, Croatia, Bosnia-Herzegovina, Macedonia (FYRM), Slovenia, Montenegro, Kosovo).

Oil Geopolitics

The geopolitics of oil and oil pipelines is crucial in the conduct of U.S.-NATO military operations. The broader Middle East-Central Asian region encompasses more than sixty percent of the World's oil reserves.

MIDDLE EAST THEATRE OF WAR

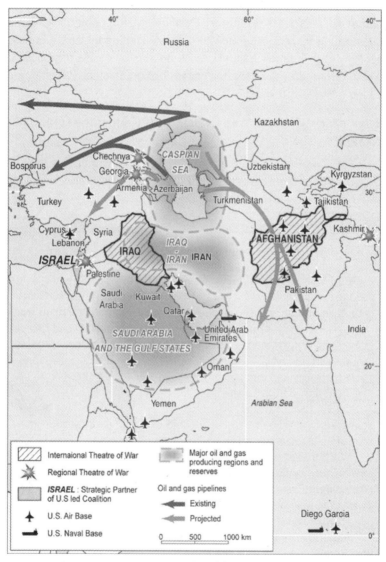

Copyright Eric Wadell, Global Research, 2001

There are at present five distinct war theaters in the Middle East-Central Asian region: *Afghanistan-Pakistan, Iraq, Palestine, Libya and Syria.* A process of military escalation could potentially lead to the merging of these separate war theaters, leading towards a broader Middle East-Central Asian war, engulfing an entire region from North Africa and the Mediterranean to Afghanistan, Pakistan and China's Western frontier.

The Legacy of World War II. Demise of Competing Imperialist powers

What is referred euphemistically as the "post war era" is in fact a period of continuous wars and militarization. This must be understood when focusing on contemporary U.S. led wars.

Corporate America Supported Nazi Germany

Corporate America neither wanted Hitler to lose this war nor to win it; instead they wanted this war to go on as long as possible. Henry Ford had initially refused to produce weapons for Great Britain, but now he changed his tune. According to his biographer, David Lanier Lewis, he "expressed the hope that neither the Allies nor the Axis would win [the war]," and he suggested that the U.S. should supply both the Allies and the Axis powers with "the tools to keep on fighting until they both collapse."

On 22 June 1941, the Wehrmacht rolled across the Soviet border, powered by Ford and GM engines and equipped with the tools produced in Germany by American capital and know-how.

While many leaders of corporate America hoped that the Nazis and the Soviets would remain locked for as long as possible in a war that would debilitate them both, thus prolonging the European war that was proving to be so profitable, the experts in Washington and London predicted that the Soviets would be crushed, "like an egg" by the Wehrmacht. The U.S.SR, however, became the first country to fight the Blitzkrieg to a standstill.

Dr. Jacques R. Pauwels, Profits über Alles! American Corporations and Hitler, Global Research, June 8, 2004.

The U.S. emerges in the wake of the Second World War unscathed. Most of the fighting was conducted by its allies, a strategy which the U.S. has used consistently in post-world war II conflicts. Moreover, a careful examination of World War II suggests that U.S. corporate interests including Rockefeller's Standard Oil supported both America's allies as well as its enemies including Nazi Germany well beyond the U.S.'s entry into World War II in December 1941. The strategic objective was to weaken both sides, namely to destabilize competing imperialist powers.

Emerging as the victor nation in the wake of World War II, the U.S. has determined the political and economic contours of post-War Western Europe. U.S. troops are stationed in several European countries. Both its World War II adversaries (Germany, Japan, Italy) as well as its allies (France, U.K. Belgium, the Netherlands) have been weakened. With the exception of the U.K. which is part of the Anglo-American axis, these countries are outgoing colonial powers, displaced by U.S. hegemony. Their pre-World War II colonial territories including Indonesia, The Congo, Indochina, Rwanda (among others) have been gradually integrated over a period of half a century into a dominant U.S. sphere of influence.

In Africa, the process of displacement of France's sphere of influence is still ongoing. The U.S. is currently taking over the control of France and Belgium's former colonies in Central Africa and West Africa. Washington also exerts a decisive role in the Maghreb. (See Chapter VIII).

"Internal Colonialism" in the European Union

A complex form of "internal colonialism" is also emerging in the European Union. U.S. financial institutions and business conglomerates together with their European partners are prevalent in setting the monetary, trade and investment agenda.

Politics are subordinated to dominant financial interests. What is also unfolding in terms of secret trade negotiations (under the TTIP and CETA), is a process of economic and political integration between the EU and North America. These agreements together with the Trans-Pacific Partnership (TPP) constitute the building blocks of a process of global economic domination.

Meanwhile, presidential and parliamentary elections in the EU, including Germany, Italy and France (for example, Sarkozy and Hollande) are increasingly the object of covert political interference by the U.S. (modeled on the "color revolutions"), namely U.S. sponsored regime change in the European Union. The fundamental question is to what extent are European leaders political proxies?

U.S. Sponsored Wars and Military-Intelligence Operations

The entire period (1945- present) has been marked by a succession of U.S. sponsored wars and military-intelligence interventions in all major regions of the World.

We are not dealing with piecemeal military operations pertaining to specific countries and regions: There is a military road-map, a sequence of military operations. Non-conventional forms of intervention including State sponsored terrorist attacks rather than theater war have also been launched.

America's war is a cohesive and coordinated plan of worldwide military conquest which serves dominant financial and corporate interests. The structure of alliances including NATO is crucial.

The European Union plays a central role in this military agenda. The member states of the EU are allies of the Anglo-American axis, but at the same time, a restructuring process is occurring within the EU, whereby previously sovereign countries are increasingly under the jurisdiction of powerful financial institutions.

The imposition of the IMF's deadly economic reforms on several European countries is indicative of America's interference in European affairs. What is at stake is a major shift in EU political and economic structures, whereby member states of the EU are de facto re-categorized by the IMF and treated in the same way as an indebted Third World country.

Military Action in Support of Economic Warfare

While the U.S. has intervened militarily in major regions of the World, the thrust of U.S. foreign policy is to have these wars fought by America's allies or to resort to non-conventional forms of warfare.

The thrust of this agenda is twofold.

1) U.S. military might is coupled with that of "Global NATO" including Israel (a de facto member of the Atlantic Alliance). We are dealing with a formidable force, in terms of advanced weapons systems. U.S. military bases have been established in all major regions of the World under the geographical command structure. A new U.S. Africa Command (AFRICOM) has been established.

2) Military action supports powerful economic and financial interests. A strategy of "Economic Warfare" under the neoliberal agenda is implemented in close coordination with military planning.

The purpose of warfare is not conquest per se. The U.S. lost the Vietnam war, but the ultimate objective to destroy Vietnam as a sovereign country was achieved. Vietnam together with Cambodia today constitute a new impoverished frontier of the global cheap labor economy.

Moreover, the countries which fought for their sovereignty against U.S. imperialism in Asia (including Vietnam, Cambodia, South Korea, Indonesia and the Philippines) have been integrated into bilateral military cooperation agreements with the Pentagon. This structure of alliances imposed on defeated nations is being used by the U.S. to foment conflict with China.

The imperial project is predicated on economic conquest, implying the confiscation and appropriation of the wealth and resources of sovereign countries. In the Middle East, successive wars have been geared towards the confiscation of oil and gas reserves.

Countries are destroyed, often transformed into territories, sovereignty is foregone, national institutions collapse, the national economy is destroyed through the imposition of "free market" reforms under the helm of the IMF, unemployment becomes rampant, social services are dismantled, wages collapse, and people are impoverished.

The ruling capitalist elites in these countries are subordinated to those of the U.S. and its allies. The nation's assets and natural resources are transferred into the hands of foreign investors through a privatization program imposed by the invading forces in coordination with the IMF and the World Bank.

The History of Nuclear Weapons: The Legacy of Hiroshima and Nagasaki

America's early nuclear weapons doctrine under the Manhattan Project was not based on The Cold War notions of "Deterrence" and "Mutual Assured Destruction" (MAD). Moreover, contemporary post Cold War U.S. nuclear doctrine is based on the notion that nuclear weapons can be used in the conventional war theater and that these weapons are "harmless to civilians".

The strategic objective in the use of both conventional and nuclear attacks has been to trigger "mass casualty producing events" resulting in tens of thousands of deaths.

This strategy first applied towards the end of World War II in Japan and Germany was to terrorize an entire nation, as a means of military conquest.

In Japan, military targets were not the main objective: the notion of "collateral damage" was used as a justification for the mass killing of civilians, under the official pretense that Hiroshima was "a military base" and that civilians were not the target.

In the words of president Harry Truman:

> We have discovered the most terrible bomb in the history of the world. ... This weapon is to be used against Japan ... [We] will use it so that military objectives and soldiers and sailors are the target and not women and children. Even if the Japs are savages, ruthless, merciless and fanatic, we as the leader of the world for the common welfare cannot drop that terrible bomb on the old capital or the new. ... The target will be a purely military one...
>
> It seems to be the most terrible thing ever discovered, but it can be made the most useful.[7]

> The World will note that the first atomic bomb was dropped on Hiroshima a military base. That was because we wished in this first attack to avoid, insofar as possible, the killing of civilians..[8]
>
> [Note: the first atomic bomb was dropped on Hiroshima on August 6, 1945; the Second on Nagasaki, on August 9, on the same day as Truman's radio speech to the Nation]

Harry Truman

Nobody within the upper echelons of the U.S. government and military believed that Hiroshima was a military base, Truman was lying to himself and to the American public.

To this day, the use of nuclear weapons against Japan in 1945 is justified as a necessary cost for bringing World War II to an end and ultimately "saving lives". Prior to Hiroshima, the U.S. extensively used fire bombs in Japan resulting in large civilian casualties. In Germany, allied forces extensively bombed and destroyed German cities in the latter part of the war targeting civilians rather than military installations.

Post-Cold War Era: Pre-emptive Nuclear Warfare

The U.S. nuclear weapons arsenal has grown considerably. In the Post-Cold War era, ArmsControl.org (April 2013) confirms that the United States:

> *possesses 5,113 nuclear warheads, including tactical, strategic, and non-deployed weapons.*[9]

According to the 2013 official New START declaration, out of more than 5113 nuclear weapons,

> *the U.S. deploys 1,654 strategic nuclear warheads* on 792 deployed ICBMs, SLBMs, and strategic bombers...

Moreover, according to The Federation of American Scientists (FAS) the U.S. possesses 500 tactical nuclear warheads, many of which are deployed in non-nuclear states including Germany, Italy, Turkey, Belgium, the Netherlands.

In the Pentagon's Nuclear Posture Review presented to the U.S. Senate in early 2002, the Bush Administration established so-called "contingency plans" for an offensive "first strike use" of nuclear weapons, not only against the "axis of evil" (Iraq, Iran, Libya, Syria and North Korea), but also against Russia and China. U.S. nuclear doctrine under the Obama administration also includes a "first strike" use of nuclear weapons against non-nuclear states.

The History of U.S. War Crimes

The notion of "mass casualty producing events" prevails to this date in U.S. military strategies. Invariably, as in the case of Syria, the civilian casualties of war committed by the aggressor are blamed on the victims. The period extending from the Korean war (1950-53) to the present is marked by a succession of U.S. sponsored theater wars (Korea, Vietnam, Cambodia, Afghanistan, Iraq, and Yugoslavia), various forms of military intervention including low intensity conflicts, "civil wars" (The Congo, Angola, Somalia, Ethiopia, Rwanda, Sudan), military coups, U.S. sponsored death squadrons and massacres (Chile, Guatemala, Honduras, Argentina, Indonesia, Thailand, Philippines), covert wars in support of Al Qaeda "freedom fighters" (Soviet-Afghan war), U.S.-NATO covert wars using Al Qaeda as foot-soldiers (Syria), U.S.-NATO sponsored humanitarian military interventions: Libya in 2011 (aerial bombings combined with support to Al Qaeda rebels).

The Vietnam War

Eight million tons of bombs (four times the amount used by the U.S. in all of World War II) were dropped indiscriminately, leaving destruction which, if laid crater to crater, would cover an area the size of the state of Maine. Eighty percent of the bombs fell on rural areas rather than military targets, leaving ten million craters. Nearly 400,000 tons of napalm was dropped on Vietnamese villages. There was no pretense of distinguishing between combatants and civilians.

The callous designation of as much as three-fourths of South Vietnam as a "free fire zone" justified the murder of virtually anyone in thousands of villages in those vast areas. ... The CIA's Phoenix program alone killed as many as 70,000 civilians who were suspected of being part of the political leadership of the Viet Cong in the south.

There was a historically unprecedented level of chemical warfare in Vietnam, including the indiscriminate spraying of nearly 20 million gallons of defoliants on one-seventh the area of South Vietnam.

Lenora Foerstel and Brian Willson, United States War Crimes, Global Research, January 26, 2002

The objective has not been to win these wars but in essence to destabilize these countries as nation states as well as impose a proxy government which acts on behalf of Western interests.

> Accounting for these various operations, the United States has attacked, directly or indirectly, some 44 countries in different regions of the developing world, since August 1945, a number of them many times ...
> The avowed objective of these military interventions has been to effect 'regime change'. The cloaks of "human rights" and of "democracy" were invariably evoked to justify what were unilateral and illegal acts."[10]

This entire "post war period" is marked by extensive war crimes resulting in the death of millions of people. What we are dealing with is a criminal U.S. foreign policy agenda. Criminalization does not pertain to one or more heads of State. It pertains to the entire State system, it's various civilian and military institutions as well as the powerful corporate interests behind the formulation of U.S. foreign policy, the Washington think tanks, the creditor institutions which finance the military machine.

Iraq: The 1991 Gulf War

In 1996, former U.S. secretary of state Madeleine Albright was asked by Lesley Stahl on the CBS Minutes' show if she thought the price of half a million dead children was worth it. She replied, "I think this is a very hard choice, but the price – we think the price is worth it."

Quoted by Ahmed Ali and Dahr Jamail, Iraq: Children Starved of Childhood, Global Research, February 15, 2008

What distinguishes the Bush and Obama administrations in relation to the historical record of U.S. sponsored crimes and atrocities, is that the concentration camps, targeted assassinations and torture chambers are now openly considered as legitimate forms of intervention, which sustain "the global war on terrorism" and support the spread of Western democracy.

U.S. sponsored crimes are not limited to the casualties of war and the physical destruction of the nation's infrastructure. Countries are destroyed, often transformed into territories, sovereignty is foregone, national institutions collapse, the national economy is destroyed through the imposition of "free market" reforms, unemployment becomes rampant, social services are dismantled, wages collapse, and people are impoverished.

In turn, the nation's assets and natural resources are transferred into the hands of foreign investors through a privatization program imposed by the invading forces

---

U.S. Sponsored Killings in Indonesia, 1965

The United States and British governments, supported by Australia, were deeply complicit in the murder of more than half a million alleged communist sympathizers in the wake of the 1965 Indonesian coup. According to professor Brad Simpson of Princeton University the U.S. and British governments did "everything in their power" to ensure that the Indonesian army would carry out the mass killings.

John Braddock, Historian says U.S. backed "efficacious terror" in 1965 Indonesian massacre, World Socialist Web Site, July 7, 2009

Renowned New York Times columnist James Reston celebrated "A gleam of light in Asia" and wrote a kid-glove version he had clearly been given. The Australian prime minister, Harold Holt, who was visiting the U.S., offered a striking example of his sense of humor: "With 500,000 to a million communist sympathizers knocked off," he said, "I think it's safe to assume a reorientation has taken place."

John Pilger, Spoils Of A Massacre, *The Guardian Weekend*, London, 14 July 2001

Destroying Internationalism: The Truman Doctrine

The broader objective of global military dominance in the wake of World War II in support of an imperial project was formulated under the Truman administration in the late 1940s at the outset of the Cold War. It was reaffirmed by U.S. President George Herbert Walker Bush in a historical 1990 address to a joint session of the U.S. Congress and the Senate in which he proclaimed a New World Order emerging from the downfall of the Berlin Wall and the disintegration of the Soviet block.

The ideological underpinnings of this agenda are to be found in what is known as the "Truman Doctrine", first formulated by foreign policy adviser George F. Kennan in a 1948 State Department brief.

What this 1948 document conveys is continuity in U.S. foreign policy, from "Containment" during The Cold War to "Pre-emptive" Warfare and "War on Terrorism". It states in polite terms that the U.S. should seek economic and strategic dominance through military means:

Furthermore, we have about 50% of the world's wealth but only 6.3% of its population. This disparity is particularly great as between ourselves and the peoples of Asia. In this situation, we cannot fail to be the object of envy and resentment. Our real task in the coming period is to *devise a pattern of relationships which will permit us to maintain this position of disparity without positive detriment to our national security. To do so, we will have to dispense with all sentimentality* and day-dreaming; and our attention will have to be concentrated everywhere on our immediate national objectives. *We need not deceive ourselves that we can afford today the luxury of altruism and world-benefaction.*

...In the face of this situation we would be better off to dispense now with a number of the concepts which have underlined our thinking with regard to the Far East. *We should dispense with the aspiration to "be liked" or to be regarded as the repository of a high-minded international altruism.* We should stop putting ourselves in the position of being our brothers' keeper and refrain from offering moral and ideological advice. *We should cease to talk about vague and– for the Far East–unreal objectives such as human rights, the raising of the living standards, and democratization. The day is not far off when we are going to have to deal in*

*straight power concepts. The less we are then hampered by
idealistic slogans, the better.*[11]

The planned disintegration of the United Nations system as an independent and influential international body has been on the drawing board of U.S. foreign policy since the inception of the United Nations in 1946. Its planned demise was an integral part of The Truman Doctrine as defined in 1948. From the very inception of the UN, Washington has sought on the one hand to control it to its advantage, while also seeking to weaken and ultimately destroy the UN system. In the words of George Kennan:

> "Occasionally, it [the United Nations] has served a useful purpose. *But by and large it has created more problems than it has solved, and has led to a considerable dispersal of our diplomatic effort. And in our efforts to use the UN majority for major political purposes we are playing with a dangerous weapon which may some day turn against us. This is a situation which warrants most careful study and foresight on our part.*
>
> *In our efforts to use the UN majority for major political purposes we are playing with a dangerous weapon which may some day turn against us. This is a situation which warrants most careful study and foresight on our part.*[12]

Although officially committed to the "international community", Washington has largely played lip service to the United Nations. Today the UN is in many regards an appendage of the U.S. State Department. Rather than undermining the UN as an institution as proposed in the late 1940s by George Kennan, the U.S. and its allies exert control over the UN Secretariat and key UN agencies.

Since Gulf War I, the UN has largely acted as a rubber stamp. It has closed its eyes to U.S. war crimes, it has implemented so-called peacekeeping operations on behalf of the Anglo-American invaders, in violation of the UN Charter. Following the de facto "dismissal" of Secretary General Boutros Boutros Ghali, both Secretary General Kofi Annan and his successor Ban Ki-moon became tools of U.S. foreign policy, taking their orders directly from Washington.

Needless to say, successive Democratic and Republican administrations, from Harry Truman to George W. Bush and Barack Obama have been involved in carrying out this *hegemonic blueprint for global domination*, which the Pentagon calls the "Long War".

Kennan's writings point to the importance of building *a dominant Anglo-American alliance* based on "good relations between our country and [the] British Empire". In today's world, this alliance largely characterizes the military axis between Washington and London, which plays a dominant role inside NATO to the detriment of Washington's European allies. Kennan also pointed to the inclusion of Canada in the Anglo-American alliance, a policy which today has largely been implemented (under NAFTA and the integration of military command structures). Canada was viewed as a go between the U.S. and Britain, as a means for the U.S. to also exert its influence in Britain's colonies, which later became part of the Commonwealth.

"Federated Europe"

A blueprint of a European Union predicated on "a weakened Germany" had also been envisaged under the Truman doctrine. George F. Kennan had envisaged the formation of a "Federated Europe" which would be based on the strengthening of the dominant Anglo-American alliance between Britain and the U.S. , the weakening of Germany as a European power and the exclusion of Russia.

Of relevance in relation to recent developments in Ukraine and Eastern Europe, Kennan explicitly pointed in his 1948 State Department brief, to "*a policy of containment of Germany, within Western Europe*". What Kennan's observations suggest is that the *U.S. should be supportive of a European Project only inasmuch as it supports U.S. hegemonic interests.*

In this regard, we recall that the Franco-German alliance largely prevailed prior to the onslaught of the March 2003 U.S.-UK invasion of Iraq, to which both France and Germany were opposed.

The 2003 invasion of Iraq was a turning point. The election of pro-U.S. political leaders (President Sarkozy in France and Chancellor Angela Merkel in Germany) was conducive to a weakening of national sovereignty, leading to the demise of the Franco-German alliance.

Today both the French president and the German Chancellor are taking their orders directly from Washington.

Moreover, in today's context, the U.S. is committed to preventing Germany and France from developing political and economic relations with Russia, which in the eyes of Washington would undermine America's hegemonic ambitions in the European Union.

Building a U.S. Sphere of Influence in East and South East Asia

The Truman Doctrine discussed above was the culmination of a post World War II U.S. military strategy initiated with the nuclear bombing of Hiroshima and Nagasaki in August 1945 and the surrender of Japan.

In East Asia, it consisted in the post-war occupation of Japan as well as the U.S. takeover of Japan's colonial Empire including South Korea (Korea was annexed to Japan under the 1910 Japan–Korea Annexation Treaty).

Following Imperial Japan's defeat in World War II, a U.S. sphere of influence throughout East and South East Asia was established in the territories of imperial Japan's "Great East Asia Co-Prosperity Sphere".

America's hegemony in Asia was largely based on establishing a sphere of influence in countries under the colonial jurisdiction of Japan, France and the Netherlands.

The U.S. sphere of influence in Asia –which was built up in the course of the 20th Century – included the Philippines (a U.S. possession which was occupied by Japan during World War II), South Korea (annexed to Japan in 1910, U.S. proxy state in the wake of World War II), Thailand (a Japanese protectorate during World War II), Indonesia (a Dutch colony occupied by Japan during World War II, which becomes a de facto U.S. proxy State following the establishment of the Suharto military dictatorship in 1965).

This U.S. sphere of influence in Asia also extended its grip into France's former colonial possessions in Indochina, including Vietnam, Laos and Cambodia, which were under Japanese military occupation during World War II.

Obama's "Pivot to Asia" which overtly threatens China is the endgame of this historical process.

The Korean War and The Truman Doctrine

The Korean War (1950-1953) was the first major military operation undertaken by the U.S. in the wake of World War II, launched at the very outset of what was euphemistically called "The Cold War". In many respects it was a continuation of World War II, whereby Korean lands under Japanese colonial occupation were, from one day to the next, handed over to a new colonial power – The United States of America. This handover of South Korea to the U.S. took place on September 8, 1945, three weeks after the surrender of Japan on August 15, 1945.

At the Potsdam Conference (July–August 1945), the U.S. and the Soviet Union agreed to dividing Korea, along the thirty-eighth parallel. There was no "Liberation" of Korea following the entry of U.S. forces. Quite the opposite.

A U.S. military government was established in South Korea on September 8, 1945. Moreover, Japanese officials in South Korea assisted the U.S. Army Military Government (U.S.AMG) (1945-48) led by General Hodge in ensuring this transition. Japanese colonial administrators in Seoul as well as their Korean police officials worked hand in glove with their new colonial masters.

From the outset, the U.S. military government refused to recognize the provisional government of the People's Republic of Korea (PRK) (in South Korea), which was committed to major social reforms including land distribution, laws protecting the rights of workers, minimum wage legislation and the reunification of North and South Korea.

The PRK was non-aligned with an anti-colonial mandate, calling for the "establishment of close relations with The United States, U.S.SR, England, and China, and positive opposition to any foreign influences interfering with the domestic affairs of the state."[13]

The PRK was abolished by military decree in September 1945 by the U.S.AMG. There was no democracy, no liberation, no independence.

While Japan was treated as a defeated Empire, South Korea was identified as a colonial territory to be administered under U.S. military rule and U.S. occupation forces.

America's handpicked appointee *Sygman Rhee* was flown into Seoul in October 1945, in General Douglas MacArthur's personal airplane.

Extensive War Crimes against the Korean People

The crimes committed by the U.S. against the people of Korea in the course of the Korean War but also in its aftermath are unprecedented in modern history.

Moreover, it is important to understand that these U.S. sponsored crimes against humanity committed in the 1950s have, over the years, contributed to setting "a pattern of killings" and U.S. human rights violations in different parts of the World.

The Korean War was also characterized by a practice of targeted assassinations of political dissidents, which was subsequently implemented by the CIA in numerous countries including Indonesia, Vietnam, Argentina, Guatemala, El Salvador, Afghanistan, Iraq.

Invariably, these targeted killings were committed on the instructions of the CIA and carried out by a U.S. sponsored proxy government or military dictatorship. More recently, targeted assassinations of civilians, "legalized" by the U.S. Congress have become, so to speak, the "New Normal".

According to I.F. Stone's "Hidden History of the Korean War" first published in 1952 (at the height of the Korean War), the U.S. deliberately sought a pretext, an act of deception, which incited the North to cross the thirty-eighth parallel ultimately leading to all-out war.

> [I. F. Stone's book] raised questions about the origin of the Korean War, made a case that the United States government manipulated the United Nations, and gave evidence that the U.S. military and South Korean oligarchy dragged out the war by sabotaging the peace talks,[14]

In Stone's account, General Douglas MacArthur "did everything possible to avoid peace".

U.S. wars of aggression are waged under the cloak of "self defense" and pre-emptive attacks. Echoing I. F. Stone's historical statement concerning General MacArthur, sixty years later U.S. President

Barack Obama and his Defense Secretary Chuck Hagel are also "*doing everything possible to avoid peace*". This pattern of inciting the enemy "to fire the first shot" is well established in U.S. military doctrine. It pertains to creating a "War Pretext Incident" which provides the aggressor a justification to intervene on the grounds of "Self- Defense". It characterized the Japanese attack on Pearl Harbor, Hawaii in 1941, triggered by deception and provocation. U.S. officials had advanced knowledge of the Japanese attack. Pearl Harbor was the justification for America's entry into World War II.

The Tonkin Gulf Incident in August 1964 was the pretext for the U.S. to wage war on North Vietnam, following the adoption of the Tonkin Gulf Resolution by the U.S. Congress, which granted President Lyndon B. Johnson the authority to wage war on Communist North Vietnam.

I. F. Stone's analysis refutes "the standard telling" ... that the Korean War was an unprovoked aggression by the North Koreans beginning on June 25, 1950, undertaken at the behest of The Soviet Union to extend the Soviet sphere of influence to the whole of Korea, completely surprising the South Koreans, the U.S., and the U.N." But was it a surprise? Could an attack by 70,000 men using at least 70 tanks launched simultaneously at four different points have been a surprise?

Stone gathers contemporary reports from South Korean, U.S. and U.N. sources documenting what was known before June 25. The head of the U.S. CIA, Rear Admiral Roscoe H. Hillenloetter, is reported to have said on the record, "that American intelligence was aware that 'conditions existed in Korea that could have meant an invasion this week or next." (p. 2) Stone writes that "America's leading military commentator, Hanson Baldwin of the New York Times, a trusted confidant of the Pentagon, reported that they [U.S. military documents] showed 'a marked buildup by the North Korean People's Army along the 38th Parallel beginning in the early days of June.' "[15] (p. 4)

How and why did U.S. President Truman so quickly decide by June 27 to commit the U.S. military to battle in South Korea? Stone makes a strong case that there were those in the U.S. government and military who saw a war in Korea and the resulting instability in East Asia as in the U.S. national interest.[16]

According to the editor of France's *Nouvel Observateur* Claude Bourdet:

> If Stone's thesis corresponds to reality, we are in the presence of the greatest swindle in the whole of military history… not a question of a harmless fraud but of a terrible maneuver in which deception is being consciously utilized to block peace at a time when it is possible.[16]

In the words of renowned American authors Leo Huberman and Paul Sweezy:

> We have come to the conclusion that [South Korean president] Syngman Rhee deliberately provoked the North Koreans in the hope that they would retaliate by crossing the parallel in force. The northerners fell neatly into the trap.[17]

On 25 June 1950, following the adoption of UN Security Council Resolution 82, General Douglas MacArthur, who headed the U.S. military government in occupied Japan was appointed Commander in Chief of the so-called United Nations Command (UNCOM). According to Bruce Cumings, the Korean War "bore a strong resemblance to the air war against Imperial Japan in the second world war and was often directed by the same U.S. military leaders" including generals Douglas MacArthur and Curtis LeMay.

While nuclear weapons were not used during the Korean War, what prevailed was the strategy of "mass killings of civilians" which had been formulated during World War II. A policy of killing innocent civilians was implemented through extensive air raids and bombings of German cities by American and British forces in the last weeks of World War II. In a bitter irony, military targets were safeguarded.

This unofficial doctrine of killing of civilians under the pretext of targeting military objectives largely characterized U.S. military actions both in the course of the Korean war as well as in its after-math. According to Bruce Cumings:

> On 12 August 1950, the U.S.AF dropped 625 tons of bombs on North Korea; two weeks later, the daily tonnage increased to some 800 tons.U.S. warplanes dropped more napalm and bombs on North Korea than they did during the whole Pacific campaign of World War II.[18]

The territories North of the thirty-eighth parallel were subjected to extensive carpet bombing, which resulted in the destruction of seventy-eight cities and thousands of villages:

> What was indelible about it [the Korean War of 1950-53] was the extraordinary destructiveness of the United States' air campaigns against North Korea, from the widespread and continuous use of firebombing (mainly with napalm), to threats to use nuclear and chemical weapons, and the destruction of huge North Korean dams in the final stages of the war. ....
> As a result, almost every substantial building in North Korea was destroyed.[19]

U.S. Major General William F. Dean "reported that most of the North Korean cities and villages he saw were either rubble or snow-covered wastelands".

General Curtis LeMay who coordinated the bombing raids against North Korea brazenly acknowledged that:

> Over a period of three years or so we killed off – what – twenty percent of the population. ... We burned down every town in North Korea and South Korea, too.[20]

According to Brian Willson:

> It is now believed that the population north of the imposed thirty-eighth Parallel lost nearly a third its population of eight to nine million people during the thirty-seven-month-long "hot" war, 1950-53, perhaps an unprecedented percentage of mortality suffered by one nation due to the belligerence of another.[21]

North Korea has been threatened of an attack with U.S. nuclear weapons for more than 60 years.

From The Truman Doctrine to the Neocons: Bill Clinton, George W. Bush and Barack Obama

There has been continuity throughout the post-World War II era, from Korea and Vietnam to the present.

The neoconservative agenda under the Bush administration should be viewed as the culmination of a (bipartisan) "Post War" foreign policy framework, which provided the basis for the planning of the contemporary wars and atrocities including the setting up of torture chambers, concentration camps and the extensive use of prohibited weapons directed against civilians.

Under Obama, this agenda has become increasingly cohesive with the legalization of extrajudicial killings of U.S. citizens under the anti-terrorist legislation, the extensive use of drone attacks against civilians, the massacres ordered by the U.S.-NATO-Israel alliance directed against Syrian and Iraqi civilians.

From Korea, Vietnam and Afghanistan, to the CIA sponsored military coups in Latin America and Southeast Asia, the objective has been to ensure U.S. military hegemony and global economic domination, as initially formulated under The Truman Doctrine.

Despite significant policy differences, successive Democratic and Republican administrations, from Harry Truman to Barack Obama have carried out this global military agenda.

This entire "post war period" is marked by extensive war crimes resulting in the death of more than twenty million people. This figure does not include those who perished as a result of poverty, starvation and disease.

The Criminalization of U.S. Foreign Policy

What we are dealing with is a criminal U.S. foreign policy agenda. Media propaganda has served to obfuscate this agenda. U.S. interventionism is invariably upheld as a humanitarian endeavor. Meanwhile, so-called "progressive leftists" and "anti-war activists" supported by corporate foundations have upheld this agenda on humanitarian grounds. (See Chapter XI)

Criminalization does not pertain to one or more hea pertains to the entire State system, it's various civiliar institutions as well as the powerful corporate interests behind the formulation of U.S. foreign policy, the Washington think tanks, the creditor institutions which finance the military machine. War crimes are the result of the criminalization of the U.S. State and foreign policy apparatus. We are not only dealing with individual war criminals, but with a process involving decision makers acting at different levels, with a mandate to carry out war crimes, following established guidelines and procedures.

What distinguishes the Bush and Obama administrations in relation to the historical record of U.S. sponsored crimes and atrocities, is that the concentration camps, targeted assassinations and torture chambers are now openly considered as legitimate forms of intervention, which sustain "the global war on terrorism" and support the spread of Western democracy.

The U.S. Supported the "Dirty War" in Latin America

U.S. Secretary of State Henry Kissinger played a behind-the-scenes role in the 1976 military coup in Argentina as well as in the formulation of Operation Condor which consisted in a coordinated campaign by U.S.-backed Latin American military governments in the 1970s and 1980s to hunt down, torture and murder tens of thousands of opponents of those regimes.

Kissinger's top deputy on Latin America, William Rogers, told him two days after the 1976 coup that:

> we've got to expect a fair amount of repression, probably a good deal of blood, in Argentina before too long.[22]

The Wars of the Twenty-first Century: From The Cold War to the "Global War on Terrorism"

The alleged mastermind behind the 9/11 terrorists attacks, Saudi-born Osama bin Laden, was recruited during the Soviet-Afghan war, ironically under the auspices of the CIA, "to fight the Soviet invaders".

From the outset of the Soviet-Afghan war in the early 1980s, the U.S. intelligence apparatus has supported the formation of the "Islamic brigades".

The Just War Theory

The "Just War" theory (*Jus ad Bellum*) has a longstanding tradition. It has been used throughout history to uphold the dominant social order and provide a justification for waging war. The "Just War" theory has served to camouflage the nature of U.S. foreign policy, while providing a human face to the invaders. In the case of Afghanistan, 9/11 played a key role in justifying the invasion. The NATO led wars on Yugoslavia, Afghanistan and Libya are considered "Just Wars", waged on humanitarian grounds under the Atlantic alliance's "Responsibility to Protect"(R2P) doctrine.

The September 11, 2001 Attacks and the Invasion of Afghanistan

September 11, 2001 provided a justification for waging a war without borders. Washington's agenda consists in extending the frontiers of the American Empire to facilitate complete U.S. corporate control, while installing within America the institutions of the Homeland Security State.

The September 11, 2001 attacks also played a crucial role in the formulation of U.S. military doctrine, namely in sustaining the legend that Al Qaeda is an enemy of the Western world when in fact it is a construct of U.S. intelligence, which is used not only as a pretext to wage war on humanitarian grounds but also *as an instrument of non-conventional warfare.*

On September 12, 2001, NATO invoked for the first time in its history "Article 5 of the Washington Treaty – its collective defense clause" declaring the 9/11 attacks on the World Trade Center (WTC) and the Pentagon "to be an attack against all NATO members."

Afghanistan was tagged, without a shred of evidence and prior to the conduct of an investigation, as the "state sponsor" of the 9/11 attacks. The invasion of Afghanistan in early October 2001 was presented as a counter-terrorism operation directed against the perpetrators of 9/11 and their state sponsors.

Trade unions, NGOs and many "progressive" intellectuals endorsed the U.S.-NATO led invasion. The events of 9/11 played a key role in gaining the support of various sectors of American society including the opponents and critics of the Bush administration's foreign policy.

The war on Afghanistan was prepared prior to 9/11. War prepa-

rations were already in an advanced stage of readiness. The green
light to wage war by the U.S. and NATO on Afghanistan was provided within twenty-four hours of the 9/11 attacks.

The press reports failed to reveal a fact which is known and acknowledged by military analysts: a major theater war cannot, under any circumstances, be planned and carried out in a matter of four to five weeks.

The legal argument used by Washington and NATO to invade
Afghanistan in early October 2001 was that the September 11 attacks
constituted an undeclared "armed attack" "from abroad" by an unnamed
foreign power, and that consequently "the laws of war" apply, allowing
the nation under attack, to strike back in the name of "self-defense".

The "Global War on Terrorism" was officially launched by the
Bush administration on September 11, 2001. On the following morning (September 12, 2001), NATO's North Atlantic Council meeting
in Brussels, adopted the following resolution:

> If it is determined that the [September 11, 2001] attack
> against the United States was directed from abroad
> [Afghanistan] against "The North Atlantic area", it shall
> be regarded as an action covered by Article 5 of the
> Washington Treaty" (see text box below).[23]

Article 5 of the Washington Treaty

The Parties agree that an armed attack against one or more of them
in Europe or North America shall be considered an attack against them
all and consequently they agree that, if such an armed attack occurs,
each of them, in exercise of the right of individual or collective self-
defence recognised by Article 51 of the Charter of the United Nations,
will assist the Party or Parties so attacked by taking forthwith, indi-
vidually and in concert with the other Parties, such action as it deems
necessary, including the use of armed force, to restore and maintain the
security of the North Atlantic area.

Any such armed attack and all measures taken as a result thereof
shall immediately be reported to the Security Council. Such measures
shall be terminated when the Security Council has taken the measures
necessary to restore and maintain international peace and security.
(source: www.nato.int)

Afghanistan was invaded on October 7, 2001 under NATO's doctrine of collective security: an attack on one member of the Atlantic Alliance is an attack on all members of Atlantic alliance. The presumption was that the U.S. had been attacked by Afghanistan on September 11, 2001, an absurd proposition.

Pre-emptive war directed against "Islamic terrorists" is required to defend the Homeland. Realities are turned upside down: America and the Western World are under attack.

In the wake of 9/11, the creation of this "outside enemy" served to obfuscate the real economic and strategic objectives behind the American-led wars in the Middle East and Central Asia, which encompass more than sixty percent of the World's oil and gas reserves.

Waged on the grounds of self-defense, the pre-emptive war is upheld as a "just war" with a humanitarian mandate.

Propaganda purports to erase the history of Al Qaeda created by the CIA, drown the truth and "kill the evidence" on how this "outside enemy" was fabricated and transformed into "Enemy Number One".

What the media does not mention is that the terrorists are paid killers, supported by the U.S. NATO and Israel.

Non-Conventional Warfare: Using Al Qaeda Rebels as the Foot Soldiers of the Western Military alliance

This strategy of using al Qaeda rebels as the foot soldiers of the Western military is of crucial significance. It has characterized U.S.-NATO interventions in Yugoslavia, Afghanistan, Libya and Syria. It is currently part of a covert agenda to destabilize Iraq by supporting Al Qaeda in Iraq and the Levant (AQIL).

The Islamic State

While Washington is accusing several countries of "harboring terrorists", America is the Number One "State Sponsor of Terrorism": The Islamic State of Iraq and al-Sham (ISIS) –which operates in both Syria and Iraq– is covertly supported and financed by the U.S. and its allies including Turkey, Saudi Arabia and Qatar. Moreover, the Islamic State of Iraq and al-Sham's Sunni caliphate project coincides with a longstanding U.S. agenda to carve up both Iraq and Syria into separate territories: A Sunni Islamist Caliphate, an Arab Shia Republic, a Republic of Kurdistan, among others.

U.S. sponsored Al Qaeda terror brigades (covertly supported by Western intelligence) have also been deployed in Mali, Niger, Nigeria, the Central African Republic, Somalia and Yemen.

The objective is to create sectarian and ethnic divisions with a view to destabilizing or fracturing sovereign countries modeled on former Yugoslavia.

Who is behind the Islamic State Project?

In a bitter irony, until July 2014, the rebels of the Islamic State, formerly known as the Islamic State of Iraq and the Levant (ISIL) were heralded as Syria's "opposition freedom fighters" committed to "restoring democracy" and unseating the secular government of Bashar al Assad.

And who was behind the jihadist insurgency in Syria?

Those who ordered the bombing campaign are those who are behind the Caliphate Project.

The Islamic State (IS) militia, which is currently the alleged target of a U.S.-NATO bombing campaign under a "counter-terrorism" mandate, was and continues to be supported covertly by the United States and its allies.

In other words, the Islamic State (IS) is a creation of U.S. intelligence with the support of Britain's MI6, Israel's Mossad, Pakistan's Inter-Services Intelligence (ISI) and Saudi Arabia's General Intelligence Presidency (GIP), Ri'āsat Al-Istikhbārāt Al-'Āmah (قساىئر الاستخباراتالعامة). Moreover, according to Israeli intelligence sources (Debka) NATO in liaison with the Turkish High Command has been involved in the recruitment of jihadist mercenaries from the outset of the Syrian crisis in March 2011.

In relation to the Syrian insurgency, the Islamic State fighters together with the Al Qaeda affiliated jihadist forces of the Al Nusrah Front are the foot soldiers of the Western military alliance. They are covertly supported by U.S.-NATO-Israel. Their mandate is to wage a terrorist insurgency against the government of Bashar al-Assad. The atrocities committed by Islamic State fighters in Iraq are similar to those committed in Syria.

As a result of media disinformation, Western public opinion is unaware that the Islamic State terrorists have from the very outset been supported by the United States and its allies.

America's Global Strike Plan: The Role of U.S. Strategic Command (U.S.STRATCOM)

Modern global warfare requires a centralized and unified command structure.

Global military operations in the post 9/11 era are coordinated out of U.S. Strategic Command Headquarters (U.S.STRATCOM) at the Offutt Air Force base in Nebraska, in liaison with the regional commands of the unified combatant commands as well as coalition command units in Israel, Turkey, the Persian Gulf and the Diego Garcia military base in the Indian Ocean.

Military planning and decision making at a country level by individual allies of U.S.-NATO as well as "partner nations" is integrated into a global military design including the weaponization of space.

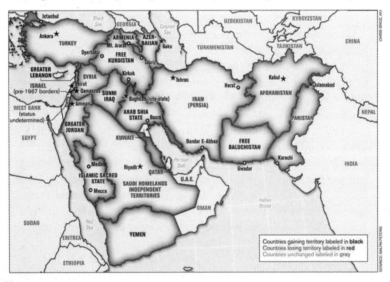

Note:
Breaking Up Countries into U.S. Proxy States: The Map of the New Middle East. In the Middle East, the redrawing of political borders is contemplated by U.S. military planners.

The following map was prepared by Lieutenant-Colonel Ralph Peters. It was published in the Armed Forces Journal in June 2006, Peters is a retired colonel of the U.S. National War Academy. (Map Copyright Lieutenant-Colonel Ralph Peters 2006). Although the map does not officially reflect Pentagon doctrine, it has been used in a training program at NATO's Defense College for senior military officers. This map, as well as other similar maps, has most probably been used at the National War Academy as well as in military planning circles.

Under its new mandate, U.S.STRATCOM has a responsibility for "overseeing a global strike plan" consisting of both conventional and nuclear weapons. In military jargon, it is slated to play the role of

> a global integrator charged with the missions of Space Operations; Information Operations; Integrated Missile Defense; Global Command & Control; Intelligence, Surveillance and Reconnaissance; Global Strike; and Strategic Deterrence...[24]

U.S.STRATCOM's responsibilities include: "leading, planning, & executing strategic deterrence operations" at a global level, "synchronizing global missile defense plans and operations", "synchronizing regional combat plans", etc. U.S.STRATCOM is the lead agency in the coordination of modern warfare.[25]

In turn, U.S. Strategic Command (U.S.STRATCOM) is in permanent liaison with the regional headquarters of the unified combat command system, which is made up of six "areas of responsibility". The regional commands are headed by a four star general who has the mandate to carry out U.S. war plans within the geographic area of responsibility. U.S. European Command (U.S.EUCOM) is responsible for military operations in Europe, Russia and Turkey. U.S.CENTCOM coordinate military operations in the Middle east and Central Asia. the jurisdiction of U.S. Pacific Command includes South Asia, South East Asia, China, Japan, Korea and Australia.

U.S. Military Deployed in 150 Countries

The U.S. military is deployed in more than 150 countries "with over 160,000 of its active-duty personnel serving outside the United States and its territories and an additional 110,000 deployed in various contingency operations."

There are approximately 68,000 U.S. troops stationed in Europe; approximately 80,000 in East Asia and the Pacific region; nearly 4,900 in North Africa, the Near East, and South Asia; over 1,750 in the Western Hemisphere; nearly 400 in Sub-Saharan Africa; and less than 100 in states of the former Soviet Union.

"Total Military Personnel and Dependent End Strength By Service, Regional Area, and Country". Defense Manpower Data Center. July 31, 2014.

The Contemporary War Theater: Towards a World War III Scenario?

In 2005, at the outset of the military deployment and build-up directed against Iran, U.S.STRATCOM was identified as "the lead Combatant Command for integration and synchronization of DoD-wide efforts in combating weapons of mass destruction."[26] (See Chapter III). The central role of U.S.STRATCOM applies to Iran and the broader Middle East as well as to China, Russia and North Korea.

Concurrently with U.S.-NATO's deployments in the Middle East directed against Syria and Iran, U.S.-NATO has been building up its weapons arsenal in Poland on Russia's Western border (Kalingrad). The deployment of U.S. forces in Poland was initiated in July 2010 (within 40 miles from the border), with a view to training Polish forces in the use of U.S. made Patriot missiles.[27] In August 2014, the Pentagon announced the deployment of U.S. troops and National Guard forces to Ukraine. U.S.-NATO is also planning further deployments of ground forces in Poland, Latvia, Estonia and Lithuania as well as in Georgia and Azerbaijan on Russia's southern border.

These deployments which are envisaged in the 2014 draft text of the "Russian Aggression Prevention Act" (RAPA) (S.2277 – 113th Congress (2013-2014)) are also part of a NATO "defensive" strategy in the case of a "Russian invasion."

Deployment on Russia's Southern border is to be coordinated under a three country agreement signed in August 2014 by Turkey, Georgia and Azerbaijan:

> Following the trilateral meeting of Azerbaijani, Turkish and Georgian defense ministers, Tbilisi announced that the three countries are interested in working out *a plan to strengthen the defense capability.*
>
> "The representatives of the governments of these three countries start to think about working out a plan to strengthen the defense capability," Alasania said, *adding that this is in the interests of Europe and NATO.*"Because, this transit route [Baku-Tbilisi-Kars] is used to transport the alliance's cargo to Afghanistan," he said.
>
> Alasania also noted that *these actions are not directed against anyone.*[28]

Russia and Obama's "Pivot to Asia"

The "Pivot to Asia" from a military standpoint consists in extending U.S. military deployments in the Asia-Pacific as well as harnessing the participation of Washington's allies in the region, including Japan, South Korea and Australia. Military preparedness under the pivot to Asia threatens China, Russia and North Horea.

These countries have signed bilateral military cooperation agreements with Washington. As U.S. allies, they are slated to be involved in Pentagon war plans directed against Russia, China and North Korea:

Japan and South Korea are also both part of a grand U.S. military project involving the global stationing of missile systems and rapid military forces, as envisioned during the Reagan Administration.[29]

In August 2014, the U.S. and Australia signed a military agreement allowing for the deployment of U.S. troops in Australia. This agreement is part of Obama's Pivot to Asia.

This Pentagon strategy of military encirclement of both China and Russia requires both *centralized military decision making* (Pentagon, U.S.STRATCOM) as well *coordination with NATO and the various U.S. regional commands.*

The Russian Federation is the World's largest country with maritime borders in the Pacific and Arctic oceans. U.S. war plans pertaining to Russia are coordinated out of U.S. Strategic Command Headquarters (U.S.STRATCOM) in Omaha, Nebraska, turn is in liaison with U.S. European Command (U.S.EUCOM) as well as the other five geographic Combat Commands.

While Russia is formally within the "jurisdiction" of U.S. European Command (U.S.EUCOM), in case of war with Russia, all three regional combat commands (U.S.EUCOM, U.S.PACOM, U.S.NORTHCOM would be involved. In practice, U.S.NORTH-COM is an extension of NORAD (North American Air Defense agreement between the U.S. and Canada). In turn the various command structures are in permanent liaison with NATO headquarters in Brussels.

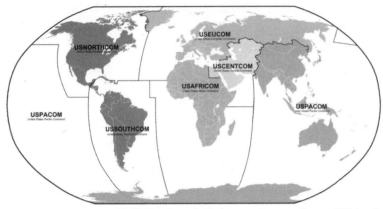

U.S. Regional Commands Source: Wikipedia

The Dangers of a Third World War

While this renewed East-West confrontation has mistakenly been labelled a "New Cold War", none of the safeguards of The Cold War era prevail.

International diplomacy has collapsed. Russia has been excluded from the Group of Eight (G-8), which has reverted to the G-7 (Group of Seven Nations). There is no "Cold War East-West dialogue" between competing superpowers geared towards avoiding military confrontation. In turn, the United Nations Security Council has become a de facto mouthpiece of the U.S. State Department.

U.S.-NATO will not, however, be able to win a conventional war against Russia, with the danger that military confrontation could lead to a nuclear war.

In the post-Cold war era, however, nuclear weapons are no longer considered as a "weapon of last resort" under the Cold War doctrine of "Mutual Assured Destruction" (MAD). Quite the opposite. nuclear weapons are heralded by the Pentagon as "harmless to the surrounding civilian population because the explosion is underground". In 2002, the U.S. Senate gave the green light for the use of nuclear weapons in the conventional war theater. Nukes are part of the "military toolbox" to be used alongside conventional weapons.

When war becomes peace, the world is turned upside down. In a bitter irony, nukes are now upheld by Washington as "instruments of peace".

The public remains largely unaware of the grave implications of these war plans. Moreover, twenty-first century military technology combines an array of sophisticated weapons systems whose destructive power would overshadow the nuclear holocausts of Hiroshima and Nagasaki. Lest we forget, the United States is the only country to have used nuclear weapons against civilians. The danger of World War III is not front-page news. The mainstream media has excluded in-depth analysis and debate on the implications of these war plans.

Notes

1. Nobel Press Release, October 9, 2009, emphasis added.
2. "Through focused, sustained engagement with partners in support of our shared security objectives". AFRICOM's area of jurisdiction extends to the entire "African continent, its island nations, and surrounding waters".
3. Project for A New American Century (PNAC), Rebuilding America's Defenses, Strategy, Forces and Resources for a New Century, Washington D.C. 2000.
4. *Ibid.*
5. See Chris Floyd, Bush's Crusade for Empire, *Global Outlook*, No. 6, November, 2003.
6. See Secret 2001 Pentagon Plan to Attack Lebanon, Global Research, July 23, 2006.
7. President Harry S. Truman, Diary, July 25, 1945.
8. President Harry S. Truman in a radio speech to the Nation, August 9, 1945.
9. ArmsControl.org, April 2013.
10. Eric Waddell, The United States' Global Military Crusade (1945-2003), Global Research, 2003.
11. George F. Kennan, 1948 State Department Brief, emphasis added.
12. *Ibid.*
13. Martin Hart-Landsberg, *Korea: Division, Reunification, & U.S. Foreign Policy.* Monthly Review Press. New York, 1998 pp. 65–6). The PRK was abolished by military decree in September 1945 by the U.S.AMG.
14. Jay Hauben, Book Review of I.F. Stone's *Hidden History of the Korean War*, OmnyNews, 2007. http://www.globalresearch.ca/the-hidden-history-of-the-korean-war/5342685.
15. *Ibid.*
16. Quoted in Stephen Lendman, "America's War on North Korea", Global Research, April 1, 2013, http://www.globalresearch.ca/americas-war-on-north-korea/5329374.
17. *Ibid.*

18. Bruce Cumings, *Korea: Forgotten Nuclear Threats*, 2005.

19. *Ibid.*

20. Quoted in Brian Willson, *Korea and the Axis of Evil*, Global Research, October 2006.

21. *Ibid.*

22. *Argentina, Declassified documents, Kissinger sought immediate support for the new military regime in spite of staff warnings on bloodshed,* National Security Archive, March 23, 2006.

23. NATO Communiqué, September 12, 2001 quoted in Michel Chossudovsky, September 11, 2001: The Crimes of War Committed "In the Name of 9/11", Global Research, http://www.globalresearch.ca/september-11-2001-the-crimes-of-war-committed-in-the-name-of-911/5311561, Perdana Global Peace Foundation, November 2012. emphasis added.

24. Defense Threat Reduction Agency and U.S. Strategic Command (U.S.TRATCOM) , http://www.dtra.mil/about/WhoWeAre.aspx.

25. *Ibid.*

26. Michel Chossudovsky, Nuclear War against Iran, Global Research, January 3, 2006.

27. *Stars and Stripes,* July 23, 2010.

28. Azeri News, August 22, 2014, emphasis added.

29. Mahdi Darius Nazemroaya, Global Military Alliance: Encircling Russia and China, Global Research, October 5, 2007.

An earlier version of this chapter was presented to the Rosa Luxemburg Conference, Berlin, January 2014

PART II

THE DANGERS
OF NUCLEAR WAR

CHAPTER II
Nuclear War and
the Future of Humanity
Conversations with Fidel Castro

From October 12 to 15, 2010, I had extensive and detailed discussions with Fidel Castro in Havana, pertaining to the dangers of nuclear war, the global economic crisis and the nature of the New World Order. These meetings resulted in a wide-ranging and fruitful interview.

The World is at a dangerous crossroads. We have reached a critical turning point in our history.

This interview with Fidel Castro provides an understanding of the nature of modern warfare: Were a military operation to be launched against Iran, the U.S. and its allies would be unable to win a conventional war, with the possibility that this war could evolve towards a nuclear war.

The details of ongoing war preparations in relation to Iran have been withheld from the public eye.

How to confront the diabolical and absurd proposition put forth by the U.S. administration that using tactical nuclear weapons against Iran will "make the World a safer place"?

A central concept put forth by Fidel Castro in the interview is the "Battle of Ideas". The leader of the Cuban Revolution believes that only a far-reaching "Battle of Ideas" could change the course of World history. The objective is to prevent the unthinkable, a nuclear war which threatens to destroy life on Earth.

The corporate media is involved in acts of camouflage. The devastating impact of a nuclear war are either trivialized or not mentioned. Against this backdrop, Fidel's message to the World must be heard; people across the land, nationally and internationally, should understand the gravity of the present situation and act forcefully at all levels of society to reverse the tide of war.

The "Battle of Ideas" is part of a revolutionary process. Against a barrage of media disinformation, Fidel Castro's resolve is to spread the word far and wide, to inform world public opinion, to "make the impossible possible", to thwart a military adventure which in the real sense of the word threatens the future of humanity. When a U.S. sponsored nuclear war becomes an "instrument of peace", condoned and accepted by the World's institutions and the highest authority including the United Nations, there is no turning back: human society has indelibly been precipitated headlong onto the path of self-destruction.

Fidel's "Battle of Ideas" must be translated into a worldwide movement. People must mobilize against this diabolical military agenda.

This war can be prevented if people pressure their governments and elected representatives, organize at the local level in towns, villages and municipalities, spread the word, inform their fellow citizens regarding the implications of a thermonuclear war, initiate debate and discussion within the armed forces.

What is required is a mass movement of people which forcefully challenges the legitimacy of war, a global people's movement which criminalizes war.

In his October 15 speech, recorded on the last day of the "Conversations" Fidel Castro warned the World on the dangers of nuclear war:

> *There would be "collateral damage", as the American political and military leaders always affirm, to justify the deaths of innocent people. In a nuclear war the "collateral damage" would be the life of all humanity. Let us have the courage to proclaim that all nuclear or conventional weapons, everything that is used to make war, must disappear!*

> *The "Battle of Ideas" consists in confronting the war criminals in high office, breaking the U.S.-led consensus in favor of a global war, changing the mindset of hundreds of millions of people, and abolishing nuclear weapons.*

> *In essence, the "Battle of Ideas" consists in restoring the truth and establishing the foundations of World Peace.*

The conventional war would be lost by the U.S. and the nuclear war is no alternative for anyone. On the other hand, nuclear war would inevitably become global.

I think nobody on Earth wishes the human species to disappear. And that is the reason why I am of the opinion that what should disappear are not just nuclear weapons, but also conventional weapons. We must provide a guarantee for peace to all peoples without distinction.

In a nuclear war the collateral damage would be the life of humankind. Let us have the courage to proclaim that all nuclear or conventional weapons, everything that is used to make war, must disappear!

It is about demanding that the world is not led into a nuclear catastrophe, it is to preserve life.

Fidel Castro Ruz, Havana, October 15, 2010.

Michel Chossudovsky: I am very honored to have this opportunity to exchange views concerning several fundamental issues affecting human society as a whole. I think that the notion that you have raised in your recent texts regarding the threat against Homo sapiens is fundamental.

What is that threat, the risk of a nuclear war and the threat to human beings, to Homo sapiens?

Fidel Castro Ruz: Since quite a long time –years I would say- but especially for some months now [2010], I began to worry about the imminence of a dangerous and probable war that could very rapidly evolve towards a nuclear war.

Before that I had concentrated all my efforts on the analysis of the capitalist system in general and the methods that the imperial tyranny has imposed on humanity. The United States applies to the world the violation of the most fundamental rights.

During the Cold War, no one spoke about war or nuclear weapons; people talked about an apparent peace, that is, between the U.S.SR and the United States, the famous MAD (Mutual Assured Destruction) was guaranteed. It seemed that the world was going to enjoy the delights of a peace that would last for an unlimited time.

Michel Chossudovsky: This notion of "mutual assured destruction" ended with The Cold War and after that the nuclear doctrine was redefined, because we never really thought about a nuclear war during the Cold War. Well, obviously, there was a danger –as even Robert McNamara said at some point in time.

But, after the Cold War, particularly after September 11 [2001], America's nuclear doctrine started to be redefined.

Fidel Castro Ruz: You asked me when was it that we became aware of the imminent risk of a nuclear war, and that dates back to the period I talked to you about previously, barely six months ago [2010]. One of the things that called our attention the most regarding such a war danger was the sinking of the Cheonan [South Korean warship] during a [joint Republic of Korea-U.S.] military maneuver. That was the flagship of the South Korean Navy; an extremely sophisticated vessel. It was at the time when we found on Global Research the journalist's report that offered a clear and truly coherent information about the sinking of the Cheonan, which could not have been the work of a submarine that had been manufactured by the U.S.SR more than sixty years ago, using an outdated technology which did not require the sophisticated equipment that could be detected by the Cheonan, during a joint maneuver with the most modern U.S. vessels.

The provocation against The Democratic People's Republic of Korea added up to our own earlier concerns about an aggression against Iran. We had been closely following the political process in that country. We knew perfectly well what happened there during the 1950s, when Iran nationalized the assets of British Petroleum [BP] in that country- which at the time was called the Anglo-Persian Oil Company.

In my opinion, the threats against Iran became imminent in June [2010], after the adoption of [United Nations Security Council] Resolution 1929 on June 9, 2010, when the United Nations Security Council condemned Iran for the research it is carrying out and the production of small amounts of twenty percent enriched uranium, and accused it of being a threat to the world.

The position adopted by each and every member of the Security Council is known: twelve member States voted in favor –five of them had the right to veto; one of them abstained and two –Brazil and Turkey- voted against. Shortly after the Resolution was adopted –the most aggressive resolution of of them all– one U.S. aircraft carrier, embedded in a combat unit, plus a nuclear submarine, went through the Suez Canal with the help of the Egyptian government. Naval units from Israel joined, heading for the Persian Gulf and the seas nearby Iran.

The sanctions imposed by the United States and its NATO allies against Iran were abusive and unjust. I cannot understand the reason why Russia and China did not veto the dangerous Resolution 1929 of the United Nations Security Council. In my opinion, this has complicated the political situation terribly and has placed the world on the brink of war.

I remember previous Israeli attacks against the Arab nuclear research centers. They first attacked and destroyed the one in Iraq in June 1981. They did not ask for anyone's permission, they did not talk to anybody; they just attacked them and the Iraqis had to endure the strikes.

In 2007, they repeated that same operation against a research center that was being built by Syria. There is something in that episode that I really don't quite understand: what was not clear to me were the underlying tactics, or the reasons why Syria did not denounce the Israeli attack against that research center where, undoubtedly, they were doing something, they were working on something for which, as it is known, they were receiving some cooperation from North Korea. That was something legal; they did not commit any violation.

I am saying this here and I am being very honest: I don't understand why this was not denounced, because, in my opinion, that would have been important. Those are two very important antecedents.

I believe there are many reasons to think that they will try to do the same against Iran: destroy its research centers or the power generation centers of that country. As is known, the power generation uranium residues are the raw material to produce plutonium.

Michel Chossudovsky: I remember that just after the Security Council's decision, with the endorsement of China and Russia, the Russian minister of Foreign Affairs said: "Well, we have approved the Resolution but that is not going to invalidate our military cooperation with Iran". That was in June [2010]. But a few months later, Moscow confirmed that military cooperation [with Iran] was going to be frozen, so now [October 2010] Iran is facing a very serious situation, because it needs Russian technology to maintain its security, namely its [S-300] air defense system.

But I think that all the threats against Russia and China are intent upon preventing the two countries from getting involved in the Iran issue. In other words, if there is a war with Iran, the other powers which are China and Russia, aren't going to intervene in any way; they will be freezing their military cooperation with Iran and therefore this is a way [for the U.S. and NATO] to extend their war in the Middle East without there being a confrontation with China and Russia and I think that this more or less is the scenario right now. There are many types of threats directed against Russia and China. The fact that China's borders are militarized –China's South Sea, the Yellow Sea, the border with Afghanistan, and also the Straits of Taiwan- it is in some way a threat to dissuade China and Russia from playing the role of powers in world geopolitics, thus paving the way and even creating consensus in favor of a war with Iran which is happening under conditions where Iran's air defense system is being weakened. [With the freeze of its military cooperation agreement with Russia] Iran is a "sitting duck" from the point of view of its ability to defend itself using its air defense system.

Fidel Castro Ruz: In my modest and serene opinion that resolution should have been vetoed. Because, in my opinion, everything has become more complicated in several ways.

Militarily, because of what you are explaining regarding, for example, the commitment that existed and the contract that had been signed to supply Iran the S-300, which are very efficient anti-aircraft weapons in the first place.

There are other things regarding fuel supplies, which are very important for China, because China is the country with the highest economic growth. Its growing economy generates greater demand for oil and gas. Even though there are agreements with Russia for oil and gas supplies, they are also developing wind energy and other forms of renewable energy. They have enormous coal reserves; nuclear energy will not increase much, only 5% for many years. In other words, the need for gas and oil in the Chinese economy is huge, and I cannot imagine, really, how they will be able to get all that energy, and at what price, if the country where they have important investments is destroyed by the U.S. But the worst risk is the very nature of that war in Iran. Iran is a Muslim country that has millions of trained combatants who are strongly motivated.

There are tens of millions of people who are under [military] orders, they are being politically educated and trained, men and women alike. There are millions of combatants trained and determined to die. These are people who will not be intimidated and who cannot be forced to changing [their behavior]. On the other hand, there are the Afghans –they are being murdered by U.S. drones– there are the Pakistanis, the Iraqis, who have seen one to two million compatriots die as a result of the anti-terrorist war invented by Bush. You cannot win a war against the Muslim world; that is sheer madness.

Michel Chossudovsky: But it's true, their conventional forces are very large, Iran can mobilize in a single day several million troops and they are on the border with Afghanistan and Iraq, and even if there is a blitzkrieg war, the U.S. cannot avoid a conventional war that is waged very close to its military bases in that region.

Fidel Castro Ruz: But the fact is that the U.S. would lose that conventional war. The problem is that nobody can win a conventional war against millions of people; they would not concentrate their forces in large numbers in a single location for the Americans to kill them.

Well, I was a guerrilla fighter and I recall that I had to think seriously about how to use the forces we had and I would never have made the mistake of concentrating those forces in a single location, because the more concentrated the forces, the greater the casualties caused by weapons of mass destruction.

Michel Chossudovsky: As you mentioned previously, a matter of utmost importance: China and Russia's decision in the Security Council, their support of Resolution 1929, is in fact harmful to them because, first, Russia cannot export weapons, thus its main source of income is now frozen. Iran was one of the main customers or buyers of Russian weapons, and that was an important source of hard currency earnings which supported Russia`s consumer goods economy thereby covering the needs of the population. And, on the other hand China requires access to sources of energy as you mentioned. The fact that China and Russia have accepted the consensus in the UN Security Council, is tantamount to saying: "We accept that you kill our economy and, in some ways, our commercial agreements with a third country". That's very serious because it [the UNSC Resolution] not only does harm to Iran; it also harms those two countries, and I suppose –even though I am not a politician –that there must be tremendous divisions within the leadership, both in Russia and in China, for that to happen, for Russia to accept not to use its veto power in the Security Council.

I spoke with Russian journalists, who told me that there wasn't exactly a consensus within the government per se; it was a guideline. But there are people in the government with a different point of view regarding the interests of Russia and its stance in the UN Security Council. How do you see this?

Fidel Castro Ruz: How do I see the general situation? The alternative in Iran –let me put it this way –the conventional war would be lost by the U.S. and the nuclear war is not an alternative for anyone.

On the other hand, nuclear war would inevitably become global. Thus the danger in my opinion exists with the current situation in Iran, bearing in mind the reasons you are presenting and many other facts; which brings me to the conclusion that the war would end up being a nuclear war.

Michel Chossudovsky: In other words, since the U.S. and its allies are unable to win the conventional war, they are going to use nuclear weapons, but that too would be a war they couldn't win, because we are going to lose everything.

Fidel Castro Ruz: Everyone would be losing that war; that would be a war that everyone would lose. What would Russia gain if a nuclear war were unleashed over there? What would China gain? What kind of war would that be? How would the world react? What effect would it have on the world economy? You explained it at the university when you spoke about the centralized defense system designed by the Pentagon. It sounds like science fiction; it doesn't even remotely resemble the last world war. The other thing which is also very important is the attempt [by the Pentagon] to transform [in terms of categorization] nuclear weapons into conventional tactical weapons.

Today, October 13th [2010], I was reading about the same thing in a news dispatch stating that the citizens of Hiroshima and Nagasaki were drawing up strong protests about the fact that the U.S.

had just carried out subcritical nuclear tests. They're called subcritical, which means the use of the nuclear weapon without deploying all the energy that might be achieved with the critical mass.

It reads: "Indignation in Hiroshima and Nagasaki because of a United States nuclear test."...

"The Japanese cities of Hiroshima and Nagasaki that suffered a nuclear attack at the end of WW II, deplored today the nuclear test carried out by the U.S. on September last, called subcritical because it does not unleash chain nuclear reactions.

"The test, the first of this kind in that country since 2006, took place on September 15th somewhere in Nevada, United States. It was officially confirmed by the Department of Energy of that country, the Japan Times informed."

What did that newspaper say?

"I deeply deplore it because I was hoping that President Barack Obama would take on the leadership in eliminating nuclear weapons", the governor of Nagasaki, Hodo Nakamura, stated today at a press conference.

A series of news items related to that follows.

"The test has also caused several protests among the citizens of Hiroshima and Nagasaki, including several survivors of the atomic bombs attacks that devastated both cities in August of 1945.

"We cannot tolerate any action of the United States that betrays President Barack Obama's promise of moving forward to a world without nuclear arms, said Yukio Yoshioka, the deputy director of the Council for the Victims of the Hiroshima Atomic Bomb.

"The government stated that it has no intention of protesting." It relegates the protest to a social level and then said: "With this, the number of subcritical nuclear tests made by the United States reaches the figure of 26, since July 1997 when the first of them took place."

Now it says:

"Washington considers that these tests do not violate the Comprehensive Nuclear Test Ban Treaty (CNTBT) since they do not unleash any chain reactions, and therefore do not release any nuclear energy, and so they can be considered to be laboratory tests."

The U.S. says that it has to make these tests because they are necessary to maintain the "security of its nuclear arsenal", which is the same as saying: since we have these great nuclear arsenals, we are doing this in order to ensure our security.

Michel Chossudovsky: Let us return to the issue of the threat against Iran, because you said that the U.S. and its allies could not win a conventional war. That is true; but nuclear weapons could be used as an alternative to conventional warfare, and this evidently is a threat against humanity, as you have emphasized in your writings.

The reason for my concern is that after The Cold War the idea of nuclear weapons with a "humanitarian face" was developed, saying that those weapons were not really dangerous, that they do not harm civilians, and in some way the nuclear weapons label was changed. Therefore, according to their criteria, [tactical] nuclear weapons are no different from conventional weapons, and now in the military manuals they say that tactical nuclear weapons are weapons that pose no harm to civilians.

Therefore, we might have a situation in which those who decide to attack Iran with a nuclear weapon would not be aware of the consequences that this might have for the Middle East, central Asia, but also for humanity as a whole, because they are going to say: "Well, according to our criteria, these [tactical] nuclear weapons [safe for civilians] are different from those deployed during The Cold War and so, we can use them against Iran as a weapon which does not [affect civilians and] does not threaten global security."

How do you view that? It's extremely dangerous, because they themselves believe their own propaganda. It is internal propaganda within the armed forces, within the political apparatus.

When tactical nuclear weapons were recategorized in 2002-2003, Senator Edward Kennedy said at that time that it was a way of blurring the boundary between conventional and nuclear weapons.

But that's where we are today; we are in an era where nuclear weapons are considered to be no different from the Kalashnikov. I'm exaggerating, but somehow nuclear weapons are now part of the tool box –that's the word they use, "tool box"– and from there you choose the type of weapon you are going to use, so the nuclear weapon could be used in the conventional war theater, leading us to the unthinkable, a nuclear war scenario on a regional level, but also with repercussions at the global level.

Fidel Castro Ruz: I heard what you said on the Round Table [Cuban TV] program about such weapons, presumably harmless to people living in the vicinity of the areas where they are to be targeted, the power [explosive yield] could range from one-third of the one that was used in Hiroshima up to six times the power [explosive yield] of that weapon, and today we know perfectly well the terrible damage it causes. One single bomb instantly killed 100,000 people. Just imagine a bomb having six times the power of that one [Hiroshima bomb], or two times that power, or an equivalent power, or 30 per cent that power. It is absurd.

There is also what you explained at the university about the attempt to present it as a humanitarian weapon that could also be available to the troops in the theater of operations. So at any given moment any commander in the theatre of operations could be authorized to use that weapon as one that was more efficient than other weapons, something that would be considered his duty according to military doctrine and the training he/she received at the military academies.

Michel Chossudovsky: In that sense, I don't think that this nuclear weapon would be used without the approval, let's say, of the Pentagon, namely its centralized command structures [for example, Strategic Command]; but I do think that it could be used without the approval of the President of the United States and Commander in Chief. In other words, it isn't quite the same logic as that which prevailed during The Cold War where there was the Red Telephone and…

Fidel Castro Ruz: I understand, Professor, what you are saying regarding the use of that weapon as authorized by the senior levels of the Pentagon, and it seems right to me that you should make that clarification so that you won't be blamed for exaggerating the dangers of that weapon.

But look, after one has learned about the antagonisms and arguments between the Pentagon and the President of the United States, there are really not too many doubts about what the Pentagon decision would be if the chief of the theater of operations requests to use that weapon because he feels it is necessary or indispensable.

Michel Chossudovsky: There is also another element. The deployment of tactical nuclear weapons now, as far as I know, is being undertaken by several European countries which belong to NATO. This is the case of Belgium, Holland, Turkey, Italy and Germany. Thus, there are plenty of these "little nuclear bombs" [mini-nukes] very close to the theater of war, and on the other hand we also have Israel.

Now then, I don't think that Israel is going to start a war on its own; that would be impossible in terms of strategy and decision-making. In modern warfare, with the centralization of communications, logistics and everything else, starting a major war would be a centralized decision. However, Israel might act if the U.S. gives Israel the green light to launch the first attack. That's within the realm of possibilities, even though there are some analysts who now say that the war on Iran will start in Lebanon and Syria with a conventional border war, and then that would provide the pretext for an escalation in military operations.

Fidel Castro Ruz: Yesterday, [October 13th 2010], a crowd of people welcomed [Iran's former president] Ahmadinejad in Lebanon like a national hero of that country. I was reading a cable about that this morning.

Besides, we also know about Israel's concerns regarding that, given the fact that the Lebanese are people with a great fighting spirit who have three times the number of reactive missiles they had in the former conflict with Israel and Lebanon, which was a great concern for Israel because they need –as the Israeli technicians have asserted – the air force to confront that weapon. And so, they state, they could only be attacking Iran for a number of hours, not three days, because they should be paying attention to such a danger. That's the reason why, from these viewpoints, every day that goes by they are more concerned, because those weapons are part of the Iranian arsenal of conventional weapons. For example, among their conventional weapons, they have hundreds of rocket launchers to fight surface warships in that area of the Caspian Sea. We know that, from the time of the Falklands war, a surface warship can dodge one, two or three rockets. But imagine how a large warship can protect itself against a shower of weapons of that kind. Those are rapid vessels operated by well-trained people, because the Iranians have been training people for thirty years now and they have developed efficient conventional weapons.

You yourself know that, and you know what happened during the last World War, before the emergence of nuclear weapons. Fifty million people died as a result of the destructive power of conventional weaponry.

A war today is not like the war that was waged in the nineteenth century, before the appearance of nuclear weapons. And wars were already highly destructive. Nuclear arms appeared at the very last minute, because Truman wanted to use them. He wanted to test the Hiroshima bomb, creating the critical mass from uranium, and the other one in Nagasaki, which created a critical mass from plutonium. The two bombs killed around 100,000 persons immediately. We don't know how many were wounded and affected by radiation, who died later on or suffered for long years from these effects. Besides, a nuclear war would create a nuclear winter.

I am talking to you about the dangers of a war, considering the immediate damage it might cause. It would be enough if we only had a limited number of them, the amount of weapons owned by one of the least mighty [nuclear] powers, India or Pakistan. Their explosion would be sufficient to create a nuclear winter from which no human being would survive. That would be impossible, since it would last for 8 to 10 years. In a matter of weeks, the sunlight would no longer be visible.

Mankind is less than 200,000 years old. So far everything was normalcy. The laws of nature were being fulfilled; the laws of life developed on planet Earth for more than 3 billion years. Men, the Homo sapiens, the intelligent beings did not exist after 8 tenths of a million years had elapsed, according to all studies.

Two hundred years ago, everything was virtually unknown. Today we know the laws governing the evolution of the species. Scientists, theologians, even the most devout religious people who initially echoed the campaign launched by the great ecclesiastical institutions against Darwinian Theory, today accept the laws of evolution as real, without it preventing their sincere practice of their religious beliefs where, quite often, people find comfort for their most heartfelt hardships.

I think nobody on Earth wishes the human species to disappear. And that is the reason why I am of the opinion that what should disappear are not just nuclear weapons, but also conventional weapons.

We must provide a guarantee for peace to all peoples without distinction, to the Iranians as well as to the Israelis.

Natural resources should be distributed. They should! I don't mean they will, or that it would be easy to do it. But there would be no other alternative for humanity, in a world of limited dimensions and resources, even if all the scientific potential to create renewable sources of energy is developed. We are almost 7 billion inhabitants, and so we need to implement a demographic policy. We need many things, and when you put them all together and you ask yourself the following question: will human beings be capable of understanding that and overcome all those difficulties? You realize that only enthusiasm can truly lead a person to say that he or she will confront and easily resolve a problem of such proportions.

Michel Chossudovsky: What you have just said is extremely important, when you spoke of Truman. Truman said that Hiroshima was a military base and that there would be no harm to civilians.

This notion of collateral damage reflects continuity in [America's] nuclear doctrine ever since the year 1945 up until today. That is, not at the level of reality but at the level of [military] doctrine and propaganda. I mean, in 1945 it was said: Let's save humanity by killing 100,000 people and deny the fact that Hiroshima was a populated city, namely that it was a military base. But nowadays the falsehoods have become much more sophisticated, more widespread, and nuclear weapons are more advanced.

So, we are dealing with the future of humanity and the threat of a nuclear war at a global level. The lies and fiction underlying [U.S.] political and military discourse would lead us to a worldwide catastrophe in which politicians would be unable to make head or tails of their own lies.

Then, you said that intelligent human beings have existed for 200,000 years, but that same intelligence, which has now been incorporated in various institutions, namely the media, the intelligence services, the United Nations, happens to be what is now going to destroy us. Because we believe in our own lies, which leads us towards nuclear war, without realizing that this would be the last war, as Einstein clearly stated. A nuclear war cannot ensure the continuation of humanity; it is a threat against the world.

Fidel Castro Ruz: Those are very good words, Professor. The collateral damage, in this case, could be humanity.

War is a crime and there is no need for any new law to describe it as such, because since Nuremberg, war has already been considered a crime, the biggest crime against humanity and peace, and the most horrible of all crimes.

Michel Chossudovsky: The Nuremberg texts clearly state: "War is a criminal act, it is the ultimate act of war, a crime against peace." This part of the Nuremberg texts is often quoted. After the Second World War, the Allies wanted to use it against those who had been defeated, and I am not saying that this is not valid, but the crimes that they committed, including the crimes committed against Germany and Japan, are never mentioned, with the use of a nuclear weapon, in the case of Japan [Hiroshima, Nagasaki].

This is an extremely important issue for me and if we are talking about a "counter-alliance for peace", the criminalization of war seems to me to be a fundamental aspect. I'm talking about the abolition of war; it is a criminal act that must be eliminated.

Fidel Castro Ruz: Well, who would judge the main criminals?

Michel Chossudovsky: The problem is that they also control the judicial system and the courts, so the judges are criminals as well. What can we do?

Fidel Castro Ruz: I say that this is part of the Battle of Ideas.

It is about demanding that the world not be spearheaded into a nuclear catastrophe, it is to preserve life.

We do not know, but we presume that if man becomes aware of his own existence, that of his people, that of his loved ones, even the U.S. military leaders would be aware of the outcome; although they are taught in life to follow orders, not infrequently genocide, as in the use of tactical or strategic nuclear weapons, because that is what they were taught in the [military] academies.

As all of this is sheer madness, no politician is exempt from the duty of conveying these truths to the people. One must believe in them, otherwise there would be nothing to fight for.

Michel Chossudovsky: I think what you are saying is that at the present time, the great debate in human history should focus on the danger of nuclear war that threatens the future of humanity, and that any discussion we have about basic needs or economics requires that we prevent the occurrence of war and instate global peace so that we can then plan living standards worldwide based on basic needs; but if we do not solve the problem of war, capitalism will not survive, right?

Fidel Castro Ruz: No, it cannot survive, in terms of all the analysis we've undertaken, it cannot survive. The capitalist system and the market economy that suffocate human life, are not going to disappear overnight, but imperialism based on force, nuclear weapons and conventional weapons with modern technology, has to disappear if we want humanity to survive.

Now, there is something occurring at this very moment which characterizes the worldwide process of disinformation, and it is the following: In Chile 33 miners were trapped 700 meters underground, and the world is rejoicing at the news that 33 miners have been saved. Well, simply, what will the world do if it becomes aware that 6,877,596,300 people need to be saved, if 33 have created universal joy and all the mass media speak only of that these days, why not save the nearly 7 billion people trapped by the terrible danger of perishing in a horrible death like those of Hiroshima or Nagasaki?

Michel Chossudovsky: This is also, clearly, the issue of media coverage that is given to different events and the propaganda emanating from the media.

I think it was an incredible humanitarian operation that the Chileans undertook, but it is true that if there is a threat to humanity, as you mentioned, it should be on the front page of every newspaper in the world because human society in its totality could be the victim of a decision that has been made, even by a three-star general who is unaware of the consequences [of nuclear weapons].

But here we are talking about how the media, particularly in the West, are hiding the most serious issue that potentially affects the world today, which is the danger of nuclear war and we must take it seriously, because both Hillary Clinton and Obama have said that they have contemplated using nuclear weapons in a so-called pre-emptive war against Iran.

Well, how do we answer? What do you say to Hillary Clinton and Barack Obama regarding their statements pertaining to the unilateral use of nuclear weapons against Iran, a country that poses no danger to anyone?

Fidel Castro Ruz: Yes, I know two things: What was discussed. This has been revealed recently, namely far-reaching arguments within the United States [National] Security Council. That is the value of the book written by Bob Woodward, because it reveals how all these discussions occurred. We know the positions of Biden, Clinton [Hillary], Obama, and indeed in those discussions, who was firmer against the extension of the war, who was able to argue with the military, it was Obama, that is a fact.

I am writing the latest reflection, actually, about that. The only one who got there, and gave him advice, who had been an opponent because of his Republican Party membership, was Colin Powell. He reminded him that he was the President of the United States, encouraging advice.

I think we should ensure that this message reaches everybody; what we have discussed. I think many people read the articles you have published on *Global Research*. I think we need to disclose, and to the extent that we have these discussions and harbor the idea of disclosure. I am delighted every time you argue, reasonably, and put forth these issues, simply, in my opinion, there is a real deficit of information for the reasons you explained.

Now, we must invent. What are the ways to make all of this known? At the time of the Twelve Apostles, there were 12 and no more, and they were given the task of disseminating the teachings a preacher transmitted to them. Sure, they had hundreds of years ahead of them. We, however, we do not have that. But I was looking at the list of personalities, and there are more than 20 prominent people who have been working with Global Research, prestigious people, asking the same questions, but they do not have hundreds of years, but, well, very little time.

Michel Chossudovsky: The anti-war movement in the United States, Canada and Europe is divided. Some people think the threat comes from Iran, others say they [the Iranians] are terrorists, and there is a lot of disinformation in the movement itself.

Besides, at the World Social Forum the issue of nuclear war is not part of the debate between people of the Left or progressives. During The Cold War there was talk of the danger of nuclear conflict, and people had this awareness.

At the last meeting held in New York [2010] on non-proliferation, under the United Nations, the emphasis was on the nuclear threat from non-state entities, from terrorists.

President Obama said that the threat comes from Al Qaeda, which has nuclear weapons. Also, if one reads Obama's speeches, what he is suggesting is that the terrorists have the ability of producing small nuclear bombs, what they call "dirty bombs". Well, it's a way of [distorting the issues] and shifting the emphasis.

Fidel Castro Ruz: That is what they tell him [Obama], that is what his own people tell him and have him believe.

Look, what do I do with the Reflections? They are distributed in the United Nations, they are sent to all the governments. The Reflections, of course, are short, and I know there are many people who read them. The problem is whether you are telling the truth or not. Of course, when one collects all this information in relation to a particular problem (because the Reflections are also summaries of on many issues) I think one has to concentrate on our part, in disclosing what is absolutely fundamental and essential, because I cannot cover everything.

Michel Chossudovsky: I have a question, because there is an important aspect related to the Cuban Revolution. In my opinion, the debate on the future of humanity is also part of a revolutionary discourse. If society as a whole were to be threatened by nuclear war, it is necessary in some form, to have a revolution at the level of ideas as well as actions against this event, [namely nuclear war].

Fidel Castro Ruz : We have to say, I repeat, that humanity is trapped 800 meters underground [reference to the Chilean mine disaster and rescue operation] and that we must get it out, we need to do a rescue operation. That is the message we must convey to a large number of people. If people in large numbers believe in that message, they will do what you are doing and they will support what you are supporting. It will no longer depend on who are those who say it, but on the fact that somebody [and eventually everybody] says it.

You have to figure out how you can reach the informed masses. The solution is not the newspapers. There is the Internet, Internet is cheaper, Internet is more accessible. I approached you through the Internet looking for news, not through news agencies, not through the press, not from CNN, but news through a newsletter I receive. Daily articles on the Internet. Over 100 pages each day.

Yesterday, you were arguing that in the United States some time ago two thirds of public opinion was against the war on Iran, and today, fifty-some percent favored military action against Iran.

Michel Chossudovsky: What happened, even in recent months, it was said: "Yes, nuclear war is very dangerous, it is a threat, but the threat comes from Iran," and there were signs in New York City saying: " Say no to nuclear Iran", and the message of these posters was to present Iran as a threat to global security, even if the threat did not exist because they do not have nuclear weapons.

Anyway, that's the situation, and The New York Times earlier this week [October 2010] published a text that says, yes, political assassinations are legal.

Then, when we have a press that gives us things like that, with the distribution that they have, it is a lot of work [on our part]. We have limited capabilities to reverse this process [of media disinformation] within the limited distribution outlets of the alternative media. In addition to that, now many of these alternative media are financed by the economic establishment.

Fidel Castro Ruz: And yet we have to fight.

Michel Chossudovsky: Yes, we keep struggling, but the message was what you said yesterday. That in the case of a nuclear war, the collateral damage would be humanity as a whole.

Fidel Castro Ruz: It would be humanity, the life of humanity.

Michel Chossudovsky: It is true that the Internet should continue to function as an outreach tool to avoid the war.

Fidel Castro Ruz: Well, it's the only way we can prevent it. If we were to create world opinion, it's like the example I mentioned: there are nearly seven billion people trapped eight hundred meters underground, we use the phenomenon of Chile to disclose these things.

Michel Chossudovsky: The comparison you make with the rescue of thirty-three miners, saying that there are thirty-three miners below ground there to be rescued, which received extensive media coverage, and you say that we have almost seven billion people that are eight hundred meters underground and do not understand what is happening, but we have to rescue them, because humanity as a whole is threatened by the nuclear weapons of the United States and its allies, because they are the ones who say they intend to use them.

Fidel Castro Ruz: And will use them [the nuclear weapons] if there is no opposition, if there is no resistance. They are deceived; they are drugged with military superiority and modern technology and do not know what they are doing.

They do not understand the consequences; they believe that the prevailing situation can be maintained. It is impossible.

Michel Chossudovsky: Or they believe that this is simply some sort of conventional weapon.

Fidel Castro Ruz: Yes, they are deluded and believe that you can still use that weapon. They believe they are in another era, they do not remember what Einstein said when he stated he did not know with what weapons World War III would be fought with, but World War IV would be fought with sticks and stones. I added there: " there wouldn't be anyone to handle the sticks and stones." That is the reality; I have it written there in the short speech you suggested I develop [broadcast worldwide on Youtube, censored by the mainstream media].

Michel Chossudovsky: The problem I see is that the use of nuclear weapons will not necessarily lead to the end of humankind from one day to the next, because the radioactive impact on human life would be gradual and cumulative.

Fidel Castro Ruz: Repeat that, please.

Michel Chossudovsky: The nuclear weapon has several different consequences: one is the explosion and destruction in the theater of war, which is the phenomenon of Hiroshima, and the other are the impacts of radiation which increase over time.

Fidel Castro Ruz: Yes, nuclear winter, as we call it. The prestigious American researcher, University of Rutgers (New Jersey) Professor Emeritus Alan Robock irrefutably showed that the outbreak of a war between two of the eight nuclear powers who possess the least amount of weapons of this kind would result in "nuclear winter".

He disclosed that at the fore of a group of researchers who used ultra-scientific computer models.

It would be enough to have 100 strategic nuclear weapons of the 25,000 possessed by the eight powers mentioned exploding in order to create temperatures below freezing all over the planet and a long night that would last approximately eight years. Professor Robock explains that it is so terrible that people are falling into a "state of denial", not wanting to think about it; it is easier to pretend that it doesn't exist". He told me that personally, at an international conference he was giving, where I had the honor of conversing with him.

Well, but I start from an assumption: If a war breaks out in Iran, it will inevitably become a nuclear war and a global war. So that's why yesterday we were saying it was not right to allow such an agreement in the Security Council, because it makes everything easier, do you see?

Such a war in Iran today would not remain confined to the local level, because the Iranians would not give in to the use of force. If it remained conventional, it would be a war the United States and Europe could not win, and I argue that it would rapidly turn into a nuclear war. If the United States were to make the mistake of using tactical nuclear weapons, there would be consternation throughout the world and the U.S. would eventually lose control of the situation.

Obama has had a heated discussion with the Pentagon about what to do in Afghanistan; imagine Obama's situation with American and Israeli soldiers fighting against millions of Iranians. The Saudis are not going to fight in Iran, nor are the Pakistanis or any other Arab or Muslim soldiers. What could happen is that the Yanks have serious conflicts with the Pakistani tribes which they are attacking and killing with their drones, and they know that. When you strike a blow against those tribes, first attacking and then warning the government, not saying anything beforehand; that is one of the things that irritates the Pakistanis. There is a strong anti-American feeling there.

It's a mistake to think that the Iranians would give up if they used tactical nuclear weapons against them, and the world really would be shocked, but then it may be too late.

Michel Chossudovsky: They cannot win a conventional war.

Fidel Castro Ruz : They cannot win.

Michel Chossudovsky: And that we can see in Iraq; in Afghanistan they can destroy an entire country, but they cannot win from a military standpoint.

Fidel Castro Ruz: But to destroy it [a country] at what price, at what cost to the world, at what economic costs, in the march towards catastrophe? The problems you mentioned are compounded, the American people would react, because the American people are often slow to react, but they react in the end. The American people react to casualties, the dead.

A lot of people supported the Nixon administration during the war in Vietnam. He even suggested the use of nuclear weapons in that country to Kissinger, who dissuaded him from taking that criminal step. The United States was obliged by the American people to end the war; it had to negotiate and had to hand over the south.

Iran would have to give up the oil in the area. In Vietnam what did they hand over? An expense. Ultimately, they are now back in Vietnam, buying oil, trading. In Iran they would lose many lives, and perhaps a large part of the oil facilities in the area would be destroyed.

In the present situation, it is likely they would not understand our message. If war breaks out, my opinion is that they, and the world, would gain nothing. If it were solely a conventional war, which is very unlikely, they would lose irretrievably, and if it becomes a global nuclear war, humanity would lose.

Michel Chossudovsky: Iran has conventional forces that are …significant.

Fidel Castro Ruz: Millions.

Michel Chossudovsky: Land forces, but also rockets and also Iran has the ability to defend itself.

Fidel Castro Ruz: If there remains one single man with a gun, this is an enemy they will have to defeat.

Michel Chossudovsky: And there are several millions with guns.

Fidel Castro Ruz: Millions, and they will have to sacrifice many American lives, unfortunately it would be only then that Americans would react, if they don't react now they will react later when it will be too late; we must write, we must divulge this as much as we can. Remember that the Christians were persecuted, they led them off to the catacombs, they killed them, they threw them to the lions, but they held on to their beliefs for centuries and later that was what they did to the Muslims, and the Muslims never yielded.

There is a real war against the Muslim world. Why are those lessons of history being forgotten? I have read many of the articles you wrote about the risks of that war.

Michel Chossudovsky: Let us return to the matter of Iran. I believe that it is very important that world opinion comprehends the war scenario. You clearly state that they would lose the war, the conventional war, they are losing it in Iraq and Afghanistan, Iran has more conventional forces than those of NATO in Afghanistan.

Fidel Castro Ruz: Much more experienced and motivated. They are now in conflict with those forces in Afghanistan and Iraq and one they don't mention: the Pakistanis of the same ethnic group as those in the resistance in Afghanistan. In White House discussions, they consider that the war is lost, that's what the book by Bob Woodward entitled "Obama's Wars" tells us. Imagine the situation if in addition to that, they append a war to liquidate whatever remains after the initial blows they inflict on Iran.

So they will be thrust into a conventional war situation that they cannot win, or they will be obliged to wage a global nuclear war, under conditions of a worldwide upheaval. And I don't know who can justify the type of war they have to wage; they have four hundred fifty targets marked out in Iran, and of these some, according to them, will have to be attacked with tactical nuclear warheads because of their location in mountainous areas and at the depth at which they are situated [underground]. Many Russian personnel and persons from other nationalities collaborating with them will die in that confrontation.

What will be the reaction of world opinion in the face of that blow which today is being irresponsibly promoted by the media with the backing of many Americans?

Michel Chossudovsky: One issue, Iran, Iraq, Afghanistan, they are all neighbouring countries in a certain way. Iran shares borders with Afghanistan and with Iraq, and the United States and NATO have military facilities in the countries they occupy. What's going to happen? I suppose that the Iranian troops are immediately going to cross the border.

Fidel Castro Ruz: Well, I don't know what tactic they're going to use, but if one were in their place, the most advisable thing to do is to not concentrate their troops, because if the troops are concentrated they will be victims of the attack with tactical nuclear weapons. In other words, in accordance with the nature of the threat as it is being described, the best thing would be for them to use a tactic similar to ours in southern Angola when we suspected that South Africa had nuclear weapons; we created tactical groups of a thousand men with land and anti-air fire power. Nuclear weapons could never –within their target range– have reached a large number of soldiers. Anti-air rocketry and other similar weapons was supporting our forces. Weapons and the conditions of the terrain change and tactics must continuously change.

Michel Chossudovsky: Dispersed.

Fidel Castro Ruz: Dispersed, but not isolated men, there were around a thousand men with appropriate weapons [within each troop formation], the terrain was sandy, wherever they went to they had to dig in and protect themselves underground, always keeping the maximum distance between the various troop formations. The enemy was never given an opportunity to aim a decisive blow against the 60,000 Cuban and Angolan soldiers in southern Angola.

What we did in that sister country is what, a thousand strong army, operating with traditional criteria, would have done. Fine, we were not one hundred thousand, in southern Angola there were sixty thousand men, Cubans and Angolans; due to technical requirements the tactical groups were mainly made up of Cubans because they handled tanks, rockets, anti-aircraft guns, communications, but the infantry was made up of Cuban and Angolan soldiers, with great fighting spirit, who didn't hesitate one second in confronting the white Apartheid army supported by the United States and Israel.

In the case of Iran, we are getting news that they are digging into the ground, and when they are asked about it, they say that they are making cemeteries to bury the invaders. I don't know if this is meant to be ironic, but I think that one would really have to dig quite a lot to protect their forces from the attack which is threatening them.

Michel Chossudovsky: Sure, but Iran has the possibility of mobilizing millions of troops.

Fidel Castro Ruz: Not just troops, but the command posts are also decisive. In my opinion, dispersion is very important. The attackers will try to prevent the transmission of orders. Every combat unit must know beforehand what they have to do under different circumstances. The attacker will try to strike and destabilize the chain of command with its radio-electronic weapons. All those factors must be kept in mind. Mankind has never experienced a similar predicament.

Anyway, Afghanistan is "a joke" and Iraq, too, when you compare them with what they are going to bump into in Iran: the weaponry, the training, the mentality, the kind of soldier... If thirty-one years ago, Iranian combatants cleaned the mine fields by advancing over them, they will undoubtedly be the most fearsome adversaries that the United States has ever come across.

The Conversations with Fidel Castro Ruz were in Spanish and took place from October 11 to 15, 2010. The above text is a shorter edited version of the Conversations with Fidel Castro Ruz focusing on the Dangers of Nuclear War.

Our thanks and appreciation to Cuba Debate for the transcription as well as the translation from Spanish.

Minor editing of English text by Michel Chossudovsky.

Fidel Castro's Message on the Dangers of Nuclear War

The use of nuclear weapons in a new war would mean the end of humanity. This was candidly foreseen by scientist Albert Einstein who was able to measure their destructive capability to generate millions of degrees of heat, which would vaporize everything within a wide radius of action. This brilliant researcher had promoted the development of this weapon so that it would not become available to the genocidal Nazi regime.

Each and every government in the world has the obligation to respect the right to life of each and every nation and of the totality of all the peoples on the planet.

Today there is an imminent risk of war with the use of that kind of weapon and I don't harbor the least doubt that an attack by the

United States and Israel against the Islamic Republic of Iran would inevitably evolve towards a global nuclear conflict.

The World's peoples have an obligation to demand of their political leaders their Right to Live. When the life of humankind, of your people and your most beloved human beings run such a risk, nobody can afford to be indifferent; not one minute can be lost in demanding respect for that right; tomorrow will be too late.

Albert Einstein himself stated unmistakably: "I do not know with what weapons World War III will be fought, but World War IV will be fought with sticks and stones". We fully comprehend what he wanted to convey, and he was absolutely right, yet in the wake of a global nuclear war, there wouldn't be anybody around to make use of those sticks and stones.

There would be "collateral damage", as the American political and military leaders always affirm, to justify the deaths of innocent people.

In a nuclear war the "collateral damage" would be the life of all humanity.

Let us have the courage to proclaim that all nuclear or conventional weapons, everything that is used to make war, must disappear!

Fidel Castro Ruz

CHAPTER III
Pre-emptive Nuclear War
The Role of Israel in Triggering
an Attack on Iran

While one can conceptualize the loss of life and destruction resulting from present-day wars including Iraq and Afghanistan, it is impossible to fully comprehend the devastation which might result from a Third World War, using "new technologies" and advanced weapons, until it occurs and becomes a reality. The international community has endorsed nuclear war in the name of world peace. "Making the world safer" is the justification for launching a military operation which could potentially result in a nuclear holocaust."

The stockpiling and deployment of advanced weapons systems directed against Iran started in the immediate wake of the 2003 bombing and invasion of Iraq. From the outset, these war plans were led by the U.S. in liaison with NATO and Israel.

Following the 2003 invasion of Iraq, the Bush administration identified Iran and Syria as the next stage of "the road map to war". U.S. military sources intimated at the time that an aerial attack on Iran could involve a large scale deployment comparable to the U.S. "shock and awe" bombing raids on Iraq in March 2003:

> American air strikes on Iran would vastly exceed the scope of the 1981 Israeli attack on the Osiraq nuclear center in Iraq, and would more resemble the opening days of the 2003 air campaign against Iraq.[1]

"Theater Iran Near Term" (TIRANNT)

Code named by U.S. military planners as TIRANNT, "Theater Iran Near Term", simulations of an attack on Iran were initiated in May 2003 "when modelers and intelligence specialists pulled together the data needed for theater-level (meaning large-scale) scenario analysis for Iran."[2]

The scenarios identified several thousand targets inside Iran as part of a "Shock and Awe" Blitzkrieg:

> The analysis, called TIRANNT, for "Theater Iran Near Term," was coupled with a mock scenario for a Marine Corps invasion and a simulation of the Iranian missile force. U.S. and British planners conducted a Caspian Sea war game around the same time. And Bush directed the U.S. Strategic Command to draw up a global strike war plan for an attack against Iranian weapons of mass destruction. All of this will ultimately feed into a new war plan for "major combat operations" against Iran that military sources confirm now [April 2006] exists in draft form.
> … Under TIRANNT, Army and U.S. Central Command planners have been examining both near-term and out-year scenarios for war with Iran, including all aspects of a major combat operation, from mobilization and deployment of forces through postwar stability operations after regime change.[3]

Different "theater scenarios" for an all-out attack on Iran had been contemplated:

> The U.S. army, navy, air force and marines have all prepared battle plans and spent four years building bases and training for "Operation Iranian Freedom". Admiral Fallon, the new head of U.S. Central Command, has inherited computerized plans under the name TIRANNT (Theatre Iran Near Term).[4]

In 2004, drawing upon the initial war scenarios under TIRANNT, Vice President Dick Cheney instructed U.S. Strategic Command (U.S.STRATCOM) to draw up a "contingency plan" of a large scale military operation directed against Iran "to be employed in response to another 9/11-type terrorist attack on the United States" on the presumption that the government in Tehran would be behind the terrorist plot. The plan included the pre-emptive use of nuclear weapons against a non-nuclear state:

> The plan includes a large-scale air assault on Iran employing both conventional and tactical nuclear weapons. Within Iran there are more than four hundred fifty major strategic targets, including numerous suspected nuclear-weapons-program development sites. Many of the targets are hardened or are deep underground and could not be taken out by conventional weapons, hence the nuclear option. As in the case of Iraq, the response is not conditional on Iran actually being involved in the act of terrorism directed against the United States. Several senior Air Force officers involved in the planning are reportedly appalled at the implications of what they are doing —that Iran is being set up for an unprovoked nuclear attack— but no one is prepared to damage his career by posing any objections.[5]

The Military Road Map: "First Iraq, then Iran"

The decision to target Iran under TIRANNT was part of the broader process of military planning and sequencing of military operations. Already under the Clinton administration, U.S. Central Command (U.S.CENTCOM) had formulated "in war theater plans" to invade first Iraq and then Iran. Access to Middle East oil was the stated strategic objective:

> The broad national security interests and objectives expressed in the President's National Security Strategy (NSS) and the Chairman's National Military Strategy (NMS) form the foundation of the United States Central Command's theater strategy. The NSS directs implementation of a strategy of dual containment of the rogue states of Iraq and Iran as long as those states pose a threat to U.S. interests, to other states in the region, and to their own citizens. Dual containment is designed to maintain the balance of power in the region without depending on either Iraq or Iran. U.S.CENTCOM's theater strategy is interest-based and threat-focused. The purpose of U.S. engagement, as espoused in the NSS, is to protect the United States' vital in-

terest in the region – uninterrupted, secure U.S./Allied access to Gulf oil.[6]

The war on Iran was viewed as part of a succession of military operations. According to (former) NATO Commander General Wesley Clark, the Pentagon's military road-map consisted of a sequence of countries:

> [The] Five-year campaign plan [includes]… a total of seven countries, beginning with Iraq, then Syria, Lebanon, Libya, Iran, Somalia and Sudan.[6] (For further details, see Chapter I)

The Role of Israel

There has been much debate regarding the role of Israel in initiating an attack against Iran.

Israel is part of a military alliance. Tel Aviv is not a prime mover. It does not have a separate and distinct military agenda.

Israel is integrated into the "war plan for major combat operations" against Iran formulated in 2006 by U.S. Strategic Command (U.S.STRATCOM). In the context of large scale military operations, an uncoordinated unilateral military action by one coalition partner, namely Israel, is from a military and strategic point almost an impossibility. Israel is a de facto member of NATO. Any action by Israel would require a "green light" from Washington.

An attack by Israel could, however, be used as "the trigger mechanism" which would unleash an all-out war against Iran, as well as retaliation by Iran directed against Israel.

In this regard, there are indications going back to the Bush administration that Washington had indeed contemplated the option of an initial (U.S. backed) attack by Israel rather than an outright U.S.-led military operation directed against Iran. The Israeli attack –although led in close liaison with the Pentagon and NATO– would have been presented to public opinion as a unilateral decision by Tel Aviv. It would then have been used by Washington to justify, in the eyes of World opinion, a military intervention of the U.S. and NATO with a view to "defending Israel", rather than attacking Iran. Under existing military cooperation agreements, both the U.S. and NATO would be "obligated" to "defend Israel" against Iran and Syria.

It is worth noting, in this regard, that at the outset of Bush's second term, (former) Vice President Dick Cheney had hinted, in no uncertain terms, that *Iran was "right at the top of the list" of the "rogue enemies"* of America, and that *Israel would, so to speak, "be doing the bombing for us"*, without U.S. military involvement and without us putting pressure on them *"to do it"*[8]

According to Cheney:

> One of the concerns people have is that Israel might do it without being asked. …Given the fact that Iran has a stated policy that their objective is the destruction of Israel, the Israelis might well decide to act first, and let the rest of the world worry about cleaning up the diplomatic mess afterwards,[9]

Commenting the Vice President's assertion, former National Security adviser Zbigniew Brzezinski in an interview on PBS, confirmed with some apprehension, yes: Cheney wants Prime Minister Ariel Sharon to act on America's behalf and "do it" for us:

> Iran I think is more ambiguous. And there the issue is certainly not tyranny; it's nuclear weapons. And the vice president today in a kind of a strange parallel statement to this declaration of freedom hinted that the Israelis may do it and in fact used language which sounds like a justification or even an encouragement for the Israelis to do it.[10]

What we are dealing with is a process of joint U.S.-NATO-Israel military planning. An operation to bomb Iran has been in the active planning stage since 2004. Officials in the Defense Department, under Bush and Obama, have been working assiduously with their Israeli military and intelligence counterparts, carefully identifying targets inside Iran. In practical military terms, any action by Israel would have to be planned and coordinated at the highest levels of the U.S. led coalition.

An attack by Israel against Iran would also require coordinated U.S.-NATO logistical support, particularly with regard to Israel's air defense system, which since January 2009 is fully integrated into that of the U.S. and NATO.[11]

Israel's X band radar system established in early 2009 with U.S. technical support has "integrate[d] Israel's missile defenses with the U.S. global missile [Space-based] detection network, which includes satellites, Aegis ships on the Mediterranean, Persian Gulf and Red Sea, and land-based Patriot radars and interceptors."[12]

What this means is that Washington ultimately calls the shots. The U.S. rather than Israel controls the air defense system:

> This is and will remain a U.S. radar system,' Pentagon spokesman Geoff Morrell said. 'So this is not something we are giving or selling to the Israelis and it is something that will likely require U.S. personnel on-site to operate.[13]

The U.S. military oversees Israel's Air Defense system, which is integrated into the Pentagon's global system. In other words, Israel cannot launch a war against Iran without Washington's consent. Hence the importance of the so-called "Green Light" legislation in the U.S. Congress sponsored by the Republican party under House Resolution 1553, which explicitly supported an Israeli attack on Iran:

> The measure, introduced by Texas Republican Louie Gohmert and 46 of his colleagues, endorses Israel's use of "all means necessary" against Iran "including the use of military force." ... "We've got to get this done. We need to show our support for Israel. We need to quit playing games with this critical ally in such a difficult area".[14]

In practice, the proposed legislation serves as a "Green Light" to the White House and the Pentagon rather than to Israel. It constitutes a rubber stamp to a U.S. sponsored war on Iran which uses Israel as a convenient military launch pad. It also serves as a justification to wage war with a view to defending Israel.

In this context, Israel could indeed provide the pretext to wage war, in response to alleged Hamas or Hezbollah attacks and/or the triggering of hostilities on the border of Israel with Lebanon. What is crucial to understand is that a minor "incident" could be used as a pretext to spark off a major military operation against Iran.

Known to U.S. military planners, Israel (rather than the U.S.A) would be the first target of military retaliation by Iran. Broadly speaking, Israelis would be the victims of the machinations of both Washington and their own government. It is, in this regard, absolutely crucial that Israelis forcefully oppose any action by the Netanyahu government to attack Iran.

Global Warfare: The Role of U.S. Strategic Command (US-TRATCOM)

In January 2005, at the outset of the military deployment and build-up directed against Iran, U.S.STRATCOM was identified as "the lead Combatant Command for integration and synchronization of DoD-wide efforts in combating weapons of mass destruction."[15] What this means is that the coordination of a large scale attack on Iran, including the various scenarios of escalation in and beyond the broader Middle East Central Asian region would be coordinated by U.S.STRATCOM. (See Chapter I).

Confirmed by military documents as well as official statements, both the U.S. and Israel contemplate the use of nuclear weapons directed against Iran. In 2006, U.S. Strategic Command (U.S.STRATCOM) announced it had achieved an operational capability for rapidly striking targets around the globe using nuclear or conventional weapons. This announcement was made after the conduct of military simulations pertaining to a U.S. led nuclear attack against a fictional country.[16]

Continuity in Relation to the Bush-Cheney Era

President Obama has largely endorsed the doctrine of pre-emptive use of nuclear weapons formulated by the previous administration. Under the 2010 Nuclear Posture Review, the Obama administration confirmed "that it is reserving the right to use nuclear weapons against Iran" for its non-compliance with U.S. demands regarding its alleged (nonexistent) nuclear weapons program.[17] The Obama administration has also intimated that it would use nukes in the case of an Iranian response to an Israeli attack on Iran. Israel has also drawn up its own "secret plans" to bomb Iran with tactical nuclear weapons:

> Israeli military commanders believe conventional strikes may no longer be enough to annihilate increasingly well-de-

> fended enrichment facilities. Several have been built be-
> neath at least 70ft of concrete and rock. However, the nu-
> clear-tipped bunker-busters would be used only if a
> conventional attack was ruled out and if the United States
> declined to intervene, senior sources said.[18]

Obama's statements on the use of nuclear weapons against Iran and North Korea are consistent with post-9/11 U.S. nuclear weapons doctrine, which allows for the use of tactical nuclear weapons in the conventional war theater.

Through a propaganda campaign which has enlisted the support of "authoritative" nuclear scientists, mini-nukes are upheld as an instrument of peace, namely a means to combating "Islamic terrorism" and instating Western style "democracy" in Iran. The low-yield nukes have been cleared for "battlefield use". They are slated to be used against Iran and Syria in the next stage of America's "War on Terrorism" alongside conventional weapons:

> Administration officials argue that low-yield nuclear
> weapons are needed as a credible deterrent against rogue
> states. [Iran, Syria, North Korea] Their logic is that existing
> nuclear weapons are too destructive to be used except in a
> full-scale nuclear war. Potential enemies realize this, thus
> they do not consider the threat of nuclear retaliation to be
> credible. However, low-yield nuclear weapons are less de-
> structive, thus might conceivably be used. That would make
> them more effective as a deterrent.[19]

The preferred nuclear weapon to be used against Iran are tactical nuclear weapons (Made in America), namely bunker buster bombs with nuclear warheads (for example, B61-11), with an explosive capacity between one third to six times a Hiroshima bomb.

The B61-11 is the "nuclear version" of the "conventional" BLU 113. or Guided Bomb Unit GBU-28. It can be delivered in much same way as the conventional bunker buster bomb.[20]

While the U.S. does not contemplate the use of strategic thermonuclear weapons against Iran, Israel's nuclear arsenal is largely composed of thermonuclear bombs which are deployed and could be used in a war with Iran. Under Israel's Jericho   III missile system with a range between 4,800 km to 6,500 km, all Iran would be within reach.

Radioactive Fallout

The issue of radioactive fallout and contamination, while casually dismissed by U.S.-NATO military analysts, would be devastating, potentially affecting a large area of the broader Middle East (including Israel) and Central Asian region.

In an utterly twisted logic, nuclear weapons are presented as a means to building peace and preventing "collateral damage". Iran's nonexistent nuclear weapons are a threat to global security, whereas those of the U.S. and Israel are instruments of peace "harmless to the surrounding civilian population."

"The Mother of All Bombs" (MOAB) Slated to be Used against Iran

Of military significance within the U.S. conventional weapons arsenal is the 21,500-pound "monster weapon" nicknamed the "mother of all bombs" The GBU-43/B or Massive Ordnance Air Blast bomb (MOAB) was categorized "as the most powerful non-nuclear weapon ever designed" with the the largest yield in the U.S. conventional arsenal. The MOAB was tested in early March 2003 before being deployed to the Iraq war theater. According to U.S. military sources, The Joint Chiefs of Staff had advised the government of Saddam Hussein prior to launching the 2003 that the "mother of all bombs" was to be used against Iraq. (There were unconfirmed reports that it had been used in Iraq).

The U.S. Department of Defense already confirmed in 2009 that it intends to use the "Mother of All Bombs" (MOAB) against Iran. The MOAB is said to be "ideally suited to hit deeply buried nuclear facilities such as Natanz or Qom in Iran"[21]. The truth of the matter is that the MOAB, given its explosive capacity, would result in significant civilian casualties. It is a conventional "killing machine" with a nuclear type mushroom cloud.

The procurement of four MOABs was commissioned in October 2009 at the hefty cost of $58.4 million, ($14.6 million for each bomb). This amount includes the costs of development and testing as well as integration of the MOAB bombs onto B-2 stealth bombers. This procurement is directly linked to war preparations in relation to Iran. The notification was contained in a ninety-three-page "reprograming memo" which included the following instructions:

> "The Department has an Urgent Operational Need (UON) *for the capability to strike hard and deeply buried targets in high threat environments.* The MOP [Mother of All Bombs] is the weapon of choice to meet the requirements of the UON [Urgent Operational Need]." It further states that *the request is endorsed by Pacific Command (which has responsibility over North Korea) and Central Command (which has responsibility over Iran).*[23]

The Pentagon is planning on a process of extensive destruction of Iran's infrastructure and mass civilian casualties through the combined use of tactical nukes and monster conventional mushroom cloud bombs, including the MOAB and the larger GBU-57A/B or Massive Ordnance Penetrator (MOP), which surpasses the MOAB in terms of explosive capacity.

The MOP is described as "a powerful new bomb aimed squarely at the underground nuclear facilities of Iran and North Korea. The gargantuan bomb–longer than eleven persons standing shoulder-to-shoulder or more than twenty feet base to nose".[24]

These are WMDs in the true sense of the word. The not so hidden objective of the MOAB and MOP, including the American nickname used to casually describe the MOAB ("Mother of all Bombs"), is "mass destruction" and mass civilian casualties with a view to instilling fear and despair.

State of the Art Weaponry: "War Made Possible Through New Technologies"

The process of U.S. military decision making in relation to Iran is supported by Star Wars, the militarization of outer space and the revolution in communications and information systems. Given the advances in military technology and the development of new weapons systems, an attack on Iran could be significantly different in terms of the mix of weapons systems, when compared to the

March 2003 *Blitzkrieg* launched against Iraq. The Iran operation is slated to use the most advanced weapons systems in support of its aerial attacks. In all likelihood, new weapons systems will be tested.

The 2000 Project for the New American Century (PNAC) document entitled Rebuilding American Defenses, outlined the mandate of the U.S. military in terms of large scale theater wars, to be waged simultaneously in different regions of the World: "*Fight and decisively win multiple, simultaneous major theater wars*". (See Chapter I)

This formulation is tantamount to a global war of conquest by a single imperial superpower. The PNAC document also called for the transformation of U.S. forces to exploit the "revolution in military affairs", namely the implementation of "war made possible through new technologies".[25] The latter consists in developing and perfecting a state of the art *global killing machine* based on an arsenal of sophisticated new weaponry, which would eventually replace the existing paradigms.

> Thus, it can be foreseen that the process of transformation will in fact be a two-stage process: *first of transition, then of more thoroughgoing transformation. The breakpoint will come when a preponderance of new weapons systems begins to enter service*, perhaps when, for example, unmanned aerial vehicles begin to be as numerous as manned aircraft. In this regard, the Pentagon should be very wary of making large investments in new programs –tanks, planes, aircraft carriers, for example– that would commit U.S. forces to current paradigms of warfare for many decades to come.[26]

The war on Iran could indeed mark this crucial break-point, with new space-based weapons systems being applied with a view to disabling an enemy which has significant conventional military capabilities including more than half a million ground forces.

Electromagnetic Weapons

Electromagnetic weapons could be used to destabilize Iran's communications systems, disable electric power generation, undermine and destabilize command and control, government infrastructure, transportation, energy, etc. Within the same family of weapons, environmental modifications techniques (ENMOD) (weather warfare) developed under the HAARP program could also be applied.[27] These weapons systems are fully operational. In this context, the U.S. Air Force document AF 2025 explicitly acknowledged the military applications of weather modification technologies:

> Weather modification will become a part of domestic and international security and could be done unilaterally. ... It could have offensive and defensive applications and even be used for deterrence purposes. The ability to generate precipitation, fog, and storms on earth or to modify space weather, improve communications through ionospheric modification (the use of ionospheric mirrors), and the production of artificial weather all are a part of an integrated set of technologies which can provide substantial increase in U.S., or degraded capability in an adversary, to achieve global awareness, reach, and power.[28]

Electromagnetic radiation enabling "remote health impairment" might also be envisaged in the war theater.[29] In turn, new uses of biological weapons by the U.S. military might also be envisaged as suggested by the PNAC: "[A]dvanced forms of biological warfare that can 'target' specific genotypes may transform biological warfare from the realm of terror to a politically useful tool."[30]

Iran's Military Capabilities: Medium and Long-range Missiles

Iran has advanced military capabilities, including medium and long-range missiles capable of reaching targets in Israel and the Gulf States. Hence the emphasis by the U.S.-NATO Israel alliance on the use of nuclear weapons, which are slated to be used either pre-emptively or in response to an Iranian retaliatory missile attack.

In November 2006, Iran tests of surface missiles two were marked by precise planning in a carefully staged operation. According to a senior American missile expert, "the Iranians demonstrated up-to-date missile-launching technology which the West had not known them to possess."[31] Israel acknowledged that "the Shehab-3, whose 2,000-km range brings Israel, the Middle East and Europe within reach".[32]

According to Uzi Rubin, former head of Israel's anti-ballistic missile program, "the intensity of the military exercise was unprecedented... It was meant to make an impression – and it made an impression."[33]

The 2006 exercises, while creating a political stir in the U.S. and Israel, did not in any way modify U.S.-NATO-Israeli resolve to wage war on Iran.

Tehran has confirmed in several statements that it will respond if it is attacked. Israel would be the immediate object of Iranian missile attacks as confirmed by the Iranian government. The issue of Israel's air defense system is therefore crucial. U.S. and allied military facilities in the Gulf states, Turkey, Saudi Arabia, Afghanistan and Iraq could also be targeted by Iran.

Iran's Ground Forces

While Iran is encircled by U.S. and allied military bases, the Islamic Republic has significant military capabilities. What is important to acknowledge is the sheer size of Iranian forces in terms of personnel (army, navy, air force) when compared to U.S. and NATO forces serving in Afghanistan and Iraq.

Confronted with a well-organized insurgency, coalition forces are already overstretched in both Afghanistan and Iraq. Would these forces be able to cope if Iranian ground forces were to enter the existing battlefield in Iraq and Afghanistan? The potential of the Resistance movement to U.S. and allied occupation would inevitably be affected.

Iranian ground forces are of the order of 700,000 of which 130,000 are professional soldiers, 220,000 are conscripts and 350,000 are reservists.[34] There are 18,000 personnel in Iran's Navy and 52,000 in the Air Force. According to the International Institute for Strategic Studies, "the Revolutionary Guards has an estimated 125,000 personnel in five branches: Its own Navy, Air Force, and Ground Forces; and the Quds Force (Special Forces)."

According to the CISS, Iran's Basij paramilitary volunteer force controlled by the Revolutionary Guards "has an estimated 90,000 active-duty full-time uniformed members, 300,000 reservists, and a total of 11 million men that can be mobilized if need be"[35], In other words, Iran can mobilize up to half a million regular troops and several million militia. Its Quds special forces are already operating inside Iraq.

U.S. Military and Allied Facilities Surrounding Iran

For several years now, Iran has been conducting its own war drills and exercises. While its Air Force has weaknesses, its intermediate and long-range missiles are fully operational. Iran's military is in a state of readiness. Iranian troop concentrations are currently within a few kilometers of the Iraqi and Afghan borders, and within proximity of Kuwait. The Iranian Navy is deployed in the Persian Gulf within proximity of U.S. and allied military facilities in the United Arab Emirates.

It is worth noting that in response to Iran's military build-up, the U.S. has been transferring large amounts of weapons to its non-NATO allies in the Persian Gulf including Kuwait and Saudi Arabia.

While Iran's advanced weapons do not measure up to those of the U.S. and NATO, Iranian forces would be in a position to inflict substantial losses to coalition forces in a conventional war theater, on the ground in Iraq or Afghanistan. Iranian ground troops and tanks in December 2009 crossed the border into Iraq without being confronted or challenged by allied forces and occupied a disputed territory in the East Maysan oil field.

Even in the event of an effective Blitzkrieg, which targets Iran's military facilities, its communications systems etc., through massive aerial bombing, using cruise missiles, conventional bunker buster bombs and tactical nuclear weapons, a war with Iran, once initiated, could eventually lead into a ground war. This is something which U.S. military planners have no doubt contemplated in their simulated war scenarios.

An operation of this nature would result in significant military and civilian casualties, particularly if nuclear weapons are used.

Within a scenario of escalation, Iranian troops could cross the border into Iraq and Afghanistan.

In turn, military escalation using nuclear weapons could lead us into a World War III scenario, extending beyond the Middle-East – Central Asian region.

In a very real sense, this military project, which has been on the Pentagon's drawing board for more than ten years, threatens the future of humanity.

Our focus in this chapter has been on war preparations. The fact that war preparations are in an advanced state of readiness does not imply that these war plans will be carried out.

The U.S.-NATO-Israel alliance realizes that the enemy has significant capabilities to respond and retaliate. This factor in itself has been crucial in the decision by the U.S. and its allies to postpone an attack on Iran.

Another crucial factor is the structure of military alliances. Whereas NATO has become a formidable force, the Shanghai Cooperation Organization (SCO), which constitutes an alliance between Russia and China and a number of former Soviet Republics has been significantly weakened.

The ongoing U.S. military threats directed against China and Russia are intended to weaken the SCO and discourage any form of military action on the part of Iran's allies in the case of a U.S. NATO Israeli attack.

Notes

1. See Target Iran – Air Strikes, Globalsecurity.org, undated.
2. William Arkin, *Washington Post,* April 16, 2006.
3. *Ibid.*
4. *New Statesman*, February 19, 2007.
5. Philip Giraldi, Deep Background,The American Conservative August 2005.
6. U.S.CENTCOM,
http://www.milnet.com/milnet/pentagon/centcom/chap1/stratgic.htm#U.S.Policy, link no longer active, archived at http://tinyurl.com/37gafu9.
7. General Wesley Clark, for further details see Chapter I.
8. See Michel Chossudovsky, Planned U.S.-Israeli Attack on Iran, Global Research, May 1, 2005.
9. Dick Cheney, quoted from an MSNBC Interview, January 2005.
10. According to Zbigniew Brzezinski.
11. Michel Chossudovsky, Unusually Large U.S. Weapons Shipment to Israel: Are the U.S. and Israel Planning a Broader Middle East War? Global Research, January 11, 2009.
12. Defense Talk.com, January 6, 2009.
13. Quoted in *Israel National News*, January 9, 2009.

14. Webster Tarpley, Fidel Castro Warns of Imminent Nuclear War; Admiral Mullen Threatens Iran; U.S.-Israel versus Iran-Hezbollah Confrontation Builds On, Global Research, August 10, 2010.

15. Michel Chossudovsky, Nuclear War against Iran, Global Research, January 3, 2006.

16. David Ruppe, Pre-emptive Nuclear War in a State of Readiness: U.S. Command Declares Global Strike Capability, Global Security Newswire, December 2, 2005.

17. U.S. Nuclear Option on Iran Linked to Israeli Attack Threat – IPS ipsnews.net, April 23, 2010.

18. Revealed: Israel plans nuclear strike on Iran – Times Online, January 7, 2007.

19. Opponents Surprised By Elimination of Nuke Research Funds, *Defense News*, November 29, 2004.

20. See Michel Chossudovsky, "Tactical Nuclear Weapons" against Afghanistan?, Global Research, December 5, 2001. See also http://www.thebulletin.org/article_nn.php?art_ofn=jf03norris.

21. Jonathan Karl, Is the U.S. Preparing to Bomb Iran? ABC News, October 9, 2009.

22. *Ibid.*

23. ABC News, *op cit*, emphasis added. To consult the reprogramming request (pdf) click here.

24. See Edwin Black, "Super Bunker-Buster Bombs Fast-Tracked for Possible Use Against Iran and North Korea Nuclear Programs", Cutting Edge, September 21, 2009.

25. See Project for a New American Century, *Rebuilding America's Defenses* Washington DC, September 2000, pdf.

26. *Ibid*, emphasis added.

27. See Michel Chossudovsky, "Owning the Weather" for Military Use, Global Research, September 27, 2004.

28. Air Force 2025 Final Report, See also U.S. Air Force: Weather as a Force Multiplier: Owning the Weather in 2025, AF2025 v3c15-1.

29. See Mojmir Babacek, Electromagnetic and Informational Weapons:, Global Research, August 6, 2004.

30. Project for a New American Century, *op cit.*, p. 60.

31. See Michel Chossudovsky, Iran's "Power of Deterrence" Global Research, November 5, 2006.

32. Debka, November 5, 2006.

33. www.cnsnews.com November 3, 2006.

34. See Islamic Republic of Iran Army – Wikipedia.

35. *Ibid.*

An earlier version of this text was first published in 2010

CHAPTER IV

The Threat of Nuclear War, North Korea or the United States?

While the Western media portrays North Korea's nuclear weapons program as a threat to Global Security, it fails to acknowledge that the U.S. has being threatening North Korea with a nuclear attack for more than half a century.

Unknown to the broader public, the U.S. had envisaged the use of nuclear weapons against North Korea at the very outset of the Korean War in 1950. In the immediate wake of the war, the U.S. deployed nuclear weapons in South Korea for use on a pre-emptive basis against the Democratic People's Republic of Korea (DPRK) in violation of the July 1953 Armistice Agreement.

"The Hiroshima Doctrine" applied to North Korea

U.S. nuclear doctrine pertaining to Korea was established following the bombings of Hiroshima and Nagasaki in August 1945, which were largely directed against civilians. (For further details see Chapter I.)

The strategic objective of a nuclear attack under the "Hiroshima doctrine" was to trigger a "mass casualty producing event" resulting in tens of thousands of deaths. The objective was to terrorize an entire nation, as a means of military conquest. Military targets were not the main objective: the notion of "collateral damage" was used as a justification for the mass killing of civilians, under the official pretense that Hiroshima was "a military base" and that civilians were not the target. (See Chapter I.)

U.S. Nuclear Weapons Stockpiled and Deployed in South Korea

Barely a few years after the end of the Korean War, the U.S. initiated its deployment of nuclear warheads in South Korea. This deployment in Uijongbu and Anyang-Ni had been envisaged as early as 1956.

It is worth noting that the U.S. decision to bring nuclear warheads to South Korea was in blatant violation of Paragraph 13(d) of the Armistice Agreement which prohibited the warring factions from introducing new weapons into Korea.

The actual deployment of nuclear warheads started in January 1958, four and a half years after the end of the Korean War, *"with the introduction of five nuclear weapon systems: the Honest John surface-to-surface missile, the Matador cruise missile, the Atomic-Demolition Munition (ADM) nuclear landmine, and the 280-mm gun and 8-inch (203mm) howitzer."*[1]

> The Davy Crockett projectile was deployed in South Korea between July 1962 and June 1968. The warhead had selective yields up to 0.25 kilotons. The projectile weighed only 34.5 kilograms (76 pounds). Nuclear bombs for fighter bombers arrived in March 1958, followed by three surface-to-surface missile systems (Lacrosse, Davy Crockett, and Sergeant) between July 1960 and September 1963. The dual-mission Nike Hercules anti-air and surface-to-surface missile arrived in January 1961, and finally the 155-mm Howitzer arrived in October 1964. At the peak of this build-up, nearly 950 warheads were deployed in South Korea.
> Four of the weapon types only remained deployed for a few years, while the others stayed for decades. The eight-inch Howitzer stayed until late 1991, the only weapon to be deployed throughout the entire thirty-three-year period of U.S. nuclear weapons deployment to South Korea. The other weapons that stayed until the end were the air delivered bombs (several different bomb types were deployed over the years, ending with the B61) and the 155-mm Howitzer nuclear artillery.[2]

Officially the U.S. deployment of nuclear weapons in South Korea lasted for thirty-three years. The deployment was targeted against North Korea as well as China and the Soviet Union.

South Korea's Nuclear Weapons Program

Concurrent and in coordination with the U.S. deployment of nuclear warheads in South Korea, the ROK had initiated its own nuclear weapons program in the early 1970s. The official story is that the U.S. exerted pressure on Seoul to abandon their nuclear weapons program and "sign the Treaty on the Non-Proliferation of Nuclear Weapons (NPT) in April 1975 before it had produced any fissile material."[3]

The ROK's nuclear initiative was from the outset in the early 1970s under the supervision of the U.S. and was developed as a component part of the U.S. deployment of nuclear weapons, with a view to threatening North Korea.

Moreover, while this program was officially ended in 1978, the U.S. promoted scientific expertise as well as training of the ROK military in the use of nuclear weapons. And bear in mind: under the ROK-U.S. CFC agreement, all operational units of the ROK are under joint command headed by a U.S. General. This means that all the military facilities and bases established by the Korean military are de facto joint facilities. There are a total of twenty-seven U.S. military facilities in the ROK.[4]

The Planning of Nuclear Attacks against North Korea from the Continental U.S. and from Strategic U.S. Submarines

According to military sources, the removal of U.S. nuclear weapons from South Korea was initiated in the mid 1970s. It was completed in 1991:

The nuclear weapons storage site at Osan Air base was deactivated in late 1977. This reduction continued over the following years and resulted in the number of nuclear weapons in South Korea dropping from some five hundred and forty in 1976 to approximately one hundred and fifty artillery shells and bombs in 1985. By the time of the Presidential Nuclear Initiative in 1991, roughly one hundred warheads remained, all of which had been withdrawn by December 1991.[5]

According to official statements, the U.S. withdrew its nuclear weapons from South Korea in December 1991.

This withdrawal from Korea did not in any way modify the U.S. threat of nuclear war directed against the DPRK. On the contrary: it was tied to changes in U.S. military strategy with regard to the deployment of nuclear warheads. Major North Korean cities were to be targeted with nuclear warheads from U.S. continental locations and from U.S. strategic submarines (SSBN) rather than military facilities in South Korea:

> After the withdrawal of [U.S.] nuclear weapons from South Korea in December 1991, the Fourth Fighter Wing at Seymour Johnson Air Force Base has been tasked with nuclear strike planning against North Korea. Since then, strike planning against North Korea with non-strategic nuclear weapons has been the responsibility of fighter wings based in the continental United States. One of these is the Fourth Fighter Wing at Seymour Johnson Air Force Base in North Carolina. …
>
> *We simulated fighting a war in Korea, using a Korean scenario. … The scenario… simulated a decision by the National Command Authority about considering using nuclear weapons. … We identified aircraft, crews, and [weapon] loaders to load up tactical nuclear weapons onto our aircraft…*
>
> With a capability to strike targets in less than fifteen minutes, the Trident D5 sea-launched ballistic missile is a *"mission critical system"* for U.S. Forces Korea. Ballistic Missile Submarines and Long-range Bombers.
>
> In addition to non-strategic air delivered bombs, sea-launched ballistic missiles onboard strategic Ohio-class submarines (SSBNs) patrolling in the Pacific appear also to have a mission against North Korea. A DOD General Inspector report from 1998 listed the Trident system as a *"mission critical system"* identified by U.S. Pacific Command and U.S. Forces Korea as *"being of particular importance to them."*
>
> Although the primary mission of the Trident system is directed against targets in Russia and China, a D5 missile launched in a low-trajectory flight provides a unique very short notice (twelve to thirteen minutes) strike capability against time-critical targets in North Korea. No other U.S. nuclear weapon system can get a warhead on target that fast. Two-thirds of SSBNs are on *"hard alert"* in the Pacific at any given time, holding Russian, Chi-

nese and North Korean targets at risk from designated patrol areas.

Long-range strategic bombers may also be assigned a nuclear strike role against North Korea although little specific is known. An Air Force map (see below) suggests a B-2 strike role against North Korea. As the designated carrier of the B61-11 earth penetrating nuclear bomb, the B-2 is a strong candidate for potential nuclear strike missions against North Korean deeply buried underground facilities.

As the designated carrier of the B61-11 earth-penetrating nuclear bomb [with an explosive capacity between one-third and six times a Hiroshima bomb] and a possible future Robust Nuclear Earth Penetrator, the B-2 stealth bomber could have an important role against targets in North Korea. Recent upgrades enable planning of a new B-2 nuclear strike mission in less than eight hours.[6]

It is worth noting that while:

the South Korean government at the time confirmed the withdrawal, U.S. affirmations were not as clear. As a result, rumors persisted for a long time –particularly in North and South Korea– that nuclear weapons remained in South Korea. Yet the withdrawal was confirmed by Pacific Command in 1998 in a declassified portion of the CINCPAC Command History for 1991.[7]

The Bush Administration's 2001 Nuclear Posture Review: Pre-emptive Nuclear War

The Bush administration in its 2001 Nuclear Posture Review established the contours of a new post 9/11 "pre-emptive" nuclear war doctrine, namely that nuclear weapons could be used as an instrument of "self-defense" against non-nuclear states. (See Chapter I.)

"*Requirements for U.S. nuclear strike capabilities*" directed against North Korea were established as part of a Global Strike mission under the helm of U.S. Strategic Command Headquarters in Omaha Nebraska, the so-called CONPLAN 8022, which was directed against a number of "rogue states" including North Korea as well as China and Russia.

> On November 18, 2005, the new Space and Global Strike command became operational at STRATCOM after passing testing in a nuclear war exercise involving North Korea.
> Current U.S. Nuclear strike planning against North Korea appears to serve three roles: The first is a vaguely defined traditional deterrence role intended to influence North Korean behavior prior to hostilities.
> This role was broadened somewhat by the 2001 Nuclear Posture Review to not only deter but also dissuade North Korea from pursuing weapons of mass destruction.
> Why, after five decades of confronting North Korea with nuclear weapons, the Bush administration believes that additional nuclear capabilities will somehow dissuade North Korea from pursuing weapons of mass destruction [nuclear weapons program] is a mystery.[8]

Who is the Threat? North Korea or the United States?

The asymmetry of nuclear weapons capabilities between the U.S. and the DPRK must be emphasized. According to ArmsControl.org (April 2013) the United States:

> *possesses 5,113 nuclear warheads, including tactical, strategic, and non-deployed weapons.*[9]

According to the official New START declaration, out of more than 5,113 nuclear weapons,

> *The U.S. deploys 1,654 strategic nuclear warheads on 792 deployed ICBMs, SLBMs, and strategic bombers...*[10]

Moreover, according to The Federation of American Scientists the U.S. possesses 500 tactical nuclear warheads.[11]

In contrast the DPRK, according to the same source:

> has separated enough plutonium for roughly 4-8 nuclear warheads. North Korea unveiled a centrifuge facility in

2010, but ability to produce highly-enriched uranium for weapons remains unclear.[12]

According to expert opinion:

> There is no evidence that North Korea has the means to lob a nuclear-armed missile at the United States or anyone else. So far, it has produced several atomic bombs and tested them, but it lacks the fuel and the technology to miniaturize a nuke and place it on a missile[13]

According to Siegfried Hecker, one of America's pre-eminent nuclear scientists:

> Despite its recent threats, North Korea does not yet have much of a nuclear arsenal because it lacks fissile materials and has limited nuclear testing experience,[14]

The threat of nuclear war does not emanate from the DPRK but from the U.S. and its allies.

The Democratic People's Republic of Korea, the unspoken victim of U.S. military aggression, has been incessantly portrayed as a warmongering nation, a menace to the American Homeland and a "threat to World Peace". These stylized accusations have become part of a media consensus.

Meanwhile, Washington is now implementing a $32 billion refurbishing of strategic nuclear weapons as well as a revamping of its tactical nuclear weapons, which according to a 2002 Senate decision *"are harmless to the surrounding civilian population."*

These continuous threats and actions of latent aggression directed against the DPRK should also be understood as part of the broader U.S. military agenda in East Asia, directed against China and Russia.

It is important that people across the land, in the U.S., Western countries, come to realize that the United States rather than North Korea or Iran is a threat to global security.

Notes

1. See The Nuclear Information Project: U.S. Nuclear Weapons in Korea.
2. *Ibid.*
3. Daniel A. Pinkston, "South Korea's Nuclear Experiments," CNS Research Story, November 9, 2004, http://cns.miis.edu.
4. See List of United States Army installations in South Korea – Wikipedia
5. The Nuclear Information Project: Withdrawal of U.S. Nuclear Weapons from South Korea, nukstrat.com/korea/withdrawal.htm.
6. *Ibid.*
7. *Ibid.*
8. *Ibid.*
9. ArmsControl.org April 2013.
10. *Ibid.*
11. *Ibid.*
12. *Ibid.*
13. North Korea: What's really happening, Salon.com April 5, 2013.
14. *Ibid.*

An earlier version of this chapter was presented at a Conference in Seoul, ROK, in June 2013 in commemoration of the sixtieth anniversary of the Armistice agreement marking the end of the Korean War.

CHAPTER V

Fukushima: A Nuclear War without a War
The Unspoken Crisis of Worldwide Nuclear Radiation

The 2011 Fukushima disaster in Japan has brought to the forefront the dangers of worldwide nuclear radiation.

The crisis in Japan has been described as "a nuclear war without a war". In the words of renowned novelist Haruki Murakami:

> This time no one dropped a bomb on us ... We set the stage, we committed the crime with our own hands, we are destroying our own lands, and we are destroying our own lives.

Nuclear radiation –which threatens life on Earth– is not front page news in comparison to the most insignificant issues of public concern, including the local level crime scene or the tabloid gossip reports on Hollywood celebrities.

While the long-term repercussions of the Fukushima Daiichi nuclear disaster are yet to be fully assessed, they are far more serious than those pertaining to the 1986 Chernobyl disaster in the Ukraine, which resulted in almost one million deaths.[1]

The shaky political consensus both in Japan, the U.S. and Western Europe is that the crisis at Fukushima was contained.

The realities, however, are otherwise. Fukushima[3] was leaking unconfirmed amounts of plutonium. According to Dr. Helen Caldicott, *"one millionth of a gram of plutonium, if inhaled can cause cancer"*.

An opinion poll in May 2011 confirmed that more than 80 per cent of the Japanese population did not believe the government's information regarding the nuclear crisis.[2]

The Impacts in Japan

The Japanese government has been obliged to acknowledge that "the severity rating of its nuclear crisis … matches that of the 1986 Chernobyl disaster". In a bitter irony, however, this tacit admission by the Japanese authorities has proven to been part of the cover-up of a significantly larger catastrophe, resulting in a process of global nuclear radiation and contamination:

> While Chernobyl was an enormous unprecedented disaster, it only occurred at one reactor and rapidly melted down. Once cooled, it was able to be covered with a concrete sarcophagus that was constructed with 100,000 workers. There are a staggering 4400 tons of nuclear fuel rods at Fukushima, which greatly dwarfs the total size of radiation sources at Chernobyl.[3]

Worldwide Contamination

The dumping of highly radioactive water into the Pacific Ocean constitutes a potential trigger to a process of global radioactive contamination. Radioactive elements have not only been detected in the food chain in Japan, radioactive rain water has been recorded in California:

> Hazardous radioactive elements being released in the sea and air around Fukushima accumulate at each step of various food chains (for example, into algae, crustaceans, small fish, bigger fish, then humans; or soil, grass, cow's meat and milk, then humans). Entering the body, these elements – called internal emitters – migrate to specific organs such as the thyroid, liver, bone, and brain, continuously irradiating small volumes of cells with high doses of alpha, beta and/or gamma radiation, and over many years often induce cancer.[4]

While the spread of radiation to the West Coast of North America has been acknowledged, the early 2011 press reports "quoting diplomatic sources" stated that only "tiny amounts of radioactive particles have arrived in California but do not pose a threat to human health."

According to the news agencies, the unnamed sources have access to data from a network of measuring stations run by the United Nations' Comprehensive Test Ban Treaty Organization. ...

Greg Jaczko, chair of the U.S. Nuclear Regulatory Commission, told White House reporters on Thursday (March 17) that his experts "don't see any concern from radiation levels that could be harmful here in the United States or any of the U.S. territories.[5]

Public Health Disaster

What prevails is a well-organized camouflage. The public health disaster in Japan, the contamination of water, agricultural land and the food chain, not to mention the broader economic and social implications, have neither been fully acknowledged nor addressed in a comprehensive and meaningful fashion by the Japanese authorities.

Japan as a nation state has been destroyed. Its landmass and territorial waters are contaminated. Part of the country is uninhabitable. High levels of radiation have been recorded in the Tokyo metropolitan area, which has a population of thirty-nine million (2010) (more than the population of Canada, circa thirty-five million (2013). There are indications that the food chain is contaminated throughout Japan:

Radioactive cesium exceeding the legal limit was detected in tea made in a factory in Shizuoka City, more than 300 kilometers away from the Fukushima Daiichi nuclear power plant. Shizuoka Prefecture is one of the most famous tea producing areas in Japan.

A tea distributor in Tokyo reported to the prefecture that it detected high levels of radioactivity in the tea shipped from the city. The prefecture ordered the factory to refrain from shipping out the product. After the accident at the Fukushima nuclear power plant, radioactive contamination of tea leaves and processed tea has been found over a wide area around Tokyo.[6]

Japan's industrial and manufacturing base is prostrate. Japan is no longer a leading industrial power. The country's exports have plummeted. The Tokyo government has announced its first trade deficit since 1980.

While the business media has narrowly centered on the impacts of power outages and energy shortages on the pace of productive activity, the broader issue pertaining to the outright radioactive contamination of the country's infrastructure and industrial base is a "scientific taboo" (that is, the radiation of industrial plants, machinery and equipment, buildings, roads, etc.).

A report released in January 2012 points to the nuclear contamination of building materials used in the construction industry, including roads and residential buildings throughout Japan.

Radioactive Ocean Water

At least three hundred tons of radioactive water continue to pour into the ocean at Fukushima every day, according to official estimates made prior to such data having been made a state secret.

To the extent they can be known, the quantities and make-up of radiation pouring out of Fukushima are also now a state secret, with independent measurement or public speculation punishable by up to ten years in prison.

Likewise, "There is no systematic testing in the U.S. of air, food and water for radiation," according to University of California (Berkeley) nuclear engineering Professor Eric Norman.

Many radioactive isotopes tend to concentrate as they pour into the air and water, so deadly clumps of Fukushima's radiation may migrate throughout the oceans for centuries to come before diffusing, which even then may not render it harmless.

Harvey Wasserman, 50 Reasons We Should Fear the Worst from Fukushima, Ecowatch.com and Global Research, February 03, 2014

The Economic Impacts of the Fukushima Disaster

A "coverup report" by the Ministry of Economy, Trade and Industry (May 2011), entitled "Economic Impact of the Great East Japan Earthquake and Current Status of Recovery" presents "Economic Recovery" as a fait accompli. It also brushes aside the issue of radiation. The impacts of nuclear radiation on the workforce and the country's industrial base are not mentioned. The report states that the distance between Tokyo-Fukushima Dai-ichi is of the order of two hundred thirty kilometers (about one hundred forty-four miles) and that the levels of radiation in Tokyo are lower than in Hong Kong and New York City.[8] This statement is made without corroborating evidence and in overt contradiction with independent radiation readings in Tokyo. In 2012, Sohgo Security Services Co. launched a lucrative "radiation measurement service targeting households in Tokyo and four surrounding prefectures".

> A [demographic] map of citizens' measured radiation levels shows radioactivity is distributed in a complex pattern reflecting the mountainous terrain and the shifting winds across a broad area of Japan north of Tokyo.
> Radiation limits begin to be exceeded at just above 0.1 microsieverts/ hour blue. Red is about fifty times the civilian radiation limit at 5.0 microsieverts/hour. Because children are much more sensitive than adults, these results are a great concern for parents of young children in potentially affected areas.[9]

The fundamental question is whether the vast array of industrial goods and components "Made in Japan" –including high-tech components, machinery, electronics, motor vehicles, etc.– and exported worldwide are contaminated?

Were this to be the case, the entire East and Southeast Asian industrial base –which depends heavily on Japanese components and industrial technology– would be affected. The potential impact on international trade would be far-reaching. In this regard, in early 2012, Russian officials confiscated irradiated Japanese automobiles and autoparts in the port of Vladivostok for sale in the Russian Federation. Needless to say, incidents of this nature in a global competitive environment, could lead to the demise of the Japanese automobile industry which is already in crisis.

While most of the automotive industry is in central Japan, Nissan's engine factory in Iwaki city is forty-two kilometers from the Fukushima Daiichi plant. Is the Nissan work force affected? Is the engine plant contaminated? The plant is within about ten to twenty kilometers of the government's "evacuation zone" from which some two hundred thousand people were evacuated.

Organized Crime and the Decontamination of Fukushima

The disaster has been sustained and aggravated by TEPCO's incompetence not to mention the corruption behind the Fukushima multi-billion decontamination program.

The coordination of the decontamination operation relied heavily on Japan's organized crime, the yakusa, which was actively involved in the recruitment of "specialized" personnel for dangerous tasks.

> The complexity of Fukushima contracts and the shortage of workers have played into the hands of the yakuza, Japan's organized crime syndicates, which have run labor rackets for generations.[10]

The Yakuza labor practices at Fukushima are based on a corrupt system of subcontracting, which does not favor the hiring of competent specialized personnel. It creates an environment of fraud and incompetence, which in the case of Fukushima could have devastating consequences. The subcontracting with organized crime syndicates is a means for major corporations involved in the clean-up to significantly reduce their labor costs.

This role of Japanese organized crime also pertains to the removal of the fuel rods from Reactor Number Four. A 2013 report documents in detail the role of Japan's Yakusa and its insidious relationship to both TEPCO as well as agencies of the Japanese government including the Ministry of Health, Labor and Welfare:

> Nearly 50 gangs with 1,050 members operate in Fukushima prefecture dominated by three major syndicates – Yamaguchi-gumi, Sumiyoshi-kai and Inagawa-kai, police say.[11]

Nuclear Energy and Nuclear War

The crisis in Japan has also brought into the open the unspoken relationship between nuclear energy and nuclear war.

Nuclear energy is not a civilian economic activity. It is an appendage of the nuclear weapons industry which is controlled by the so-called defense contractors. The powerful corporate interests behind nuclear energy and nuclear weapons overlap.

Both the media and the governments are complacent with regard to the hazards of nuclear radiation emanating from the nuclear energy industry as well as from the potential use of nuclear weapons.

In both cases, the devastating health impacts of nuclear radiation are casually denied.

Notes

1. New Book Concludes – Chernobyl death toll: 985,000, mostly from cancer Global Research, September 10, 2010. See also Matthew Penney and Mark Selden The Severity of the Fukushima Daiichi Nuclear Disaster: Comparing Chernobyl and Fukushima, Global Research, May 25, 2011.
2. Quoted in Sherwood Ross, Fukushima: Japan's Second Nuclear Disaster, Global Research, November 10, 2011.
3. Extremely High Radiation Levels in Japan: University Researchers Challenge Official Data, Global Research, April 11, 2011.
4. Helen Caldicott, Fukushima: Nuclear Apologists Play Shoot the Messenger on Radiation, *The Age*, April 26, 2011.
5. Straight.com, March 18, 20111 http://www.straight.com/news/japan-nuclear-radiation-reaches-us-west-coast-no-health-risk-reports-say.
6. More Companies Detect Radiation In Their Tea Above Legal Limits Over 300 KM From Fukushima, June 15, 2011.
7. See FUKU.S.HIMA: Radioactive Houses and Roads in Japan. Radioactive Building Materials Sold to over 200 Construction Companies, January 2012.
8. Japan's Ministry of Economy, Trade and Industry, Impact of the Great East Japan Earthquake and Current Status of Recovery, p 15, Tokyo, 2012.
9. Map of citizens' measured radiation levels
10. Reuters, October 25, 2013.
11. Special Report: Help wanted in Fukushima: Low pay, high risks and gangsters, Reuters, October 25, 2013.

PART III

U.S.-NATO Sponsored Terrorism and "Regime Change" The Destabilization of Sovereign Countries

CHAPTER VI

NATO's War on Yugoslavia Kosovo "Freedom Fighters" Financed by Organized Crime

NATO's aerial bombardment of Yugoslavia started on March 24, 1999. The bombings which lasted for almost three months, were followed by the military invasion (under a bogus UN mandate) and illegal occupation of the province of Kosovo.

At the outset of the War, NATO had reassured World opinion that "precise targeting" using smart bombs was intended to avoid "collateral damage" including environmental hazards:

> *We do everything we possibly can to avoid unnecessary collateral damage. We take it very seriously, work very hard at doing that, spend a lot of time planning for the missions.[1]*

Early in the air campaign, NATO chose to bomb Belgrade's children's hospital. It had been singled out by military planners as a strategic target.

NATO nonetheless acknowledged that the bombing was undertaken to "save the lives" of newly born babies. They did not target the section of the hospital where the babies were residing, instead they targeted the hospital building which housed the power generator for the entire hospital, which meant no electricity for the incubators, which meant that the entire hospital was evacuated and many of the children died.

I visited that hospital and interviewed the director of the hospital, one year after the bombing in June 2000 and saw with my own eyes how this operation had been carried out with utmost accuracy.

These war crimes were selectively implemented using NATO's "smart bombs". In Yugoslavia, the civilian economy was the target: hospitals, airports, government buildings, manufacturing, infrastructure, not to mention seventeenth century churches and the country's historical and cultural heritage.

Heralded by the global media as a humanitarian peace-keeping mission, NATO's ruthless 1999 bombing of Belgrade and Pristina goes far beyond the breach of international law. While Slobodan Milosevic was demonized, portrayed as a remorseless dictator, the Kosovo Liberation Army (KLA) was upheld as a self-respecting nationalist movement struggling for the rights of ethnic Albanians. The truth of the matter is that the KLA was sustained by organized crime with the tacit approval of the United States and its allies.

Following a pattern set during the War in Bosnia, public opinion had been carefully misled. The multibillion dollar Balkans narcotics trade had played a crucial role in "financing the conflict" in Kosovo in accordance with Western economic, strategic and military objectives. Amply documented by European police files, acknowledged by numerous studies, the links of the Kosovo Liberation Army (KLA) to criminal syndicates in Albania, Turkey and the European Union were known to Western governments and intelligence agencies since the mid-1990s.

> The financing of the Kosovo guerilla war poses critical questions and it sorely test claims of an "ethical" foreign policy. Should the West back a guerilla army that appears to partly financed by organized crime.[1]

While KLA leaders were shaking hands with U.S. Secretary of State Madeleine Albright at Rambouillet, Europol (the European Police Organization based in the Hague) was "preparing a report for European interior and justice ministers on a connection between the KLA and Albanian drug gangs."[2] In the meantime, the rebel army had been skillfully heralded by the global media (in the months preceding the NATO bombings) as broadly representative of the interests of ethnic Albanians in Kosovo.

With KLA leader Hashim Thaci (a twenty-nine year old "freedom fighter") appointed as chief negotiator at Rambouillet, the KLA had become the de facto helmsman of the peace process on behalf of the ethnic Albanian majority and this despite its links to the drug trade. The West was relying on its KLA puppets to rubber-stamp an agreement which would have transformed Kosovo into an occupied territory under Western Administration.

Ironically Robert Gelbard, America's special envoy to Bosnia, had described the KLA in 1998 as "terrorists". Christopher Hill, America's chief negotiator and architect of the Rambouillet agreement "has also been a strong critic of the KLA for its alleged dealings in drugs."[3] Moreover, two months before Rambouillet [in 1998], the U.S. State Department had acknowledged (based on reports from the U.S. Observer Mission) the role of the KLA in terrorizing and uprooting ethnic Albanians:

> The KLA harass or kidnap anyone who comes to the police, ... KLA representatives had threatened to kill villagers and burn their homes if they did not join the KLA [a process which has continued since the NATO bombings]... [T]he KLA harassment has reached such intensity that residents of six villages in the Stimlje region are ready to flee.[4]

While backing a "freedom movement" with links to the drug trade, the West was also intent on bypassing the civilian Kosovo Democratic League and its leader Ibrahim Rugova who had called for an end to the bombings and expressed his desire to negotiate a peaceful settlement with the Yugoslav authorities.[5]

Covert Financing of "Freedom Fighters"

Remember Oliver North and the Contras? The pattern in Kosovo was similar to other CIA covert operations in Central America, Haiti and Afghanistan where "freedom fighters" were financed through the laundering of drug money. Since the onslaught of the Cold War, Western intelligence agencies have developed a complex relationship to the illegal narcotics trade. In case after case, drug money laundered in the international banking system has financed covert operations.

According to author Alfred McCoy, the pattern of covert financing was established in the Indochina war. In the 1960s, the Meo army in Laos was funded by the narcotics trade as part of Washington's military strategy against the combined forces of the neutralist government of Prince Souvanna Phouma and the Pathet Lao.[6]

The pattern of drug politics set in Indochina has since been replicated in Central America and the Caribbean. "The rising curve of cocaine imports to the U.S.", wrote journalist John Dinges "followed almost exactly the flow of U.S. arms and military advisers to Central America."[7]

The military in Guatemala and Haiti, to which the CIA provided covert support, were known to be involved in the trade of narcotics into Southern Florida. And as revealed in the Iran-Contra and Bank of Commerce and Credit International (BCCI) scandals, there was strong evidence that covert operations were funded through the laundering of drug money. "Dirty money" recycled through the banking system –often through an anonymous shell company– became "covert money," used to finance various rebel groups and guerilla movements including the Nicaraguan Contras and the Afghan Mujahideen. According to a 1991 *Time Magazine* report:

> Because the U.S. wanted to supply the mujehadeen rebels in Afghanistan with stinger missiles and other military hardware it needed the full cooperation of Pakistan. By the mid-1980s, the CIA operation in Islamabad was one of the largest U.S. intelligence stations in the World. 'If BCCI is such an embarrassment to the U.S. that forthright investigations are not being pursued it has a lot to do with the blind eye the U.S. turned to the heroin trafficking in Pakistan', said a U.S. intelligence officer.[8]

America and Germany join Hands

Since the early 1990s, Bonn and Washington joined hands in establishing their respective spheres of influence in the Balkans. Their intelligence agencies had actively collaborated. Covert support to the Kosovo rebel army was established as a joint endeavor between the CIA and Germany's *Bundes Nachrichten Dienst* (BND) (which previously played a key role in installing a right wing nationalist government under Franjo Tudjman in Croatia).[9] The task to create and finance the KLA was initially given to Germany: "They used German uniforms, East German weapons and were financed, in part, with drug money."[10] The CIA was, subsequently instrumental in training and equipping the KLA in Albania.[11]

The covert activities of Germany's BND were consistent with Bonn's intent to expand its *"Lebensraum"* into the Balkans. Prior to the onset of the civil war in Bosnia in 1991, Germany and its Foreign

Minister Hans-Dietrich Genscher had actively supported secession; it had "forced the pace of international diplomacy" and pressured its Western allies to recognize Slovenia and Croatia. According to the Geopolitical Drug Watch, both Germany and the U.S. favored (although not officially) the formation of a "Greater Albania" encompassing Albania, Kosovo and parts of Macedonia.[12] According to Sean Gervasi, Germany was seeking a free hand among its allies "to pursue economic dominance in the whole of *Mitteleuropa.*"[13]

Islamic Fundamentalism in Support of the KLA

Bonn and Washington's "hidden agenda" consisted in triggering nationalist liberation movements in Bosnia and Kosovo with the ultimate purpose of destabilizing Yugoslavia. The latter objective was also carried out "by turning a blind eye" to the influx of mercenaries and financial support from Islamic fundamentalist organizations.[14]

Mercenaries financed by Saudi Arabia and Kuwait had been fighting in Bosnia.[15] And the Bosnian pattern was replicated in Kosovo: Mujahideen mercenaries from various Islamic countries were reported to be fighting alongside the KLA in Kosovo. German, Turkish and Afghan instructors were reported to be training the KLA in guerilla and diversion tactics.[16]

Financial support from Islamic countries to the KLA had been channelled through the former Albanian chief of the National Information Service (NIS), Bashkim Gazidede.[17] "Gazidede, reportedly a devout Moslem who fled Albania in March of 1997, had been investigated for his contacts with Islamic terrorist organizations."[18]

The supply route for arming KLA "freedom fighters" were the rugged mountainous borders of Albania with Kosovo and Macedonia. Albania is also a key point of transit of the Balkans drug route which supplies Western Europe with grade four heroin. Seventy-five percent of the heroin entering Western Europe is from Afghanistan via Turkey. And a large part of drug shipments originating in Turkey transits through the Balkans. According to the U.S. Drug Enforcement Administration (DEA), "it is estimated that four to six metric tons of heroin leave each month from Turkey having [through the Balkans] as destination Western Europe."[19] A recent intelligence report by Germany's Federal Criminal Agency suggests that: "Ethnic Albanians are now the most prominent group in the distribution of heroin in Western consumer countries."[20]

The Laundering of Dirty Money

In order to thrive, the criminal syndicates involved in the Balkans narcotics trade need friends in high places. Smuggling rings with alleged links to the Turkish State are said to control the trafficking of heroin through the Balkans "cooperating closely with other groups with which they have political or religious ties" including criminal groups in Albania and Kosovo.[21] In this new global financial environment, powerful undercover political lobbies connected to organized crime cultivate links to prominent political figures and officials of the military and intelligence establishment.

The narcotics trade nonetheless uses respectable banks to launder large amounts of dirty money. While comfortably removed from the smuggling operations per se, powerful banking interests in Turkey but mainly those in financial centers in Western Europe discretely collect fat commissions in a multi-billion dollar money laundering operation. These interests have high stakes in ensuring a safe passage of drug shipments into Western European markets.

The Albanian Connection

Arms smuggling from Albania into Kosovo and Macedonia started in 1992, when the Democratic Party came to power, headed by President Sali Berisha. An expansive underground economy and cross-border trade had unfolded. A triangular trade in oil, arms and narcotics had developed largely as a result of the embargo imposed by the international community on Serbia and Montenegro and the blockade enforced by Greece against Macedonia.

Industry and agriculture in Kosovo were spearheaded into bankruptcy following the IMF's lethal "economic medicine" imposed on Belgrade in 1990. The embargo was imposed on Yugoslavia. Ethnic Albanians and Serbs were driven into abysmal poverty. Economic collapse created an environment which fostered the progress of illicit trade. In Kosovo, the rate of unemployment increased to a staggering seventy percent (according to Western sources).

Poverty and economic collapse served to exacerbate simmering ethnic tensions. Thousands of unemployed youths "barely out of their Teens" from an impoverished population, were drafted into the ranks of the KLA.[22]

In neighboring Albania, the free market reforms adopted since 1992 had created conditions which favored the criminalization of State institutions. Drug money was also laundered in the Albanian "pyramids" (ponzi schemes) which mushroomed during the government of President Sali Berisha (1992-1997).[23] These shady investment funds were an integral part of the economic reforms inflicted by Western creditors on Albania.

Drug barons in Kosovo, Albania and Macedonia (with links to the Italian mafia) had become the new economic elites, often associated with Western business interests. In turn, the financial proceeds of the trade in drugs and arms were recycled towards other illicit activities (and vice versa) including a vast prostitution racket between Albania and Italy. Albanian criminal groups operating in Milan, "have become so powerful running prostitution rackets that they have even taken over the Calabrians in strength and influence."[24]

The application of "strong economic medicine" under the guidance of the Washington based Bretton Woods institutions had contributed to wrecking Albania's banking system and precipitating the collapse of the Albanian economy. The resulting chaos enabled American and European transnationals to carefully position themselves. Several Western oil companies including Occidental, Shell and British Petroleum had their eyes riveted on Albania's abundant and unexplored oil deposits. Western investors were also gawking Albania's extensive reserves of chrome, copper, gold, nickel and platinum... The Adenauer Foundation had been lobbying in the background on behalf of German mining interests.[25]

Berisha's Minister of Defense Safet Zoulali (alleged to have been involved in the illegal oil and narcotics trade) was the architect of the agreement with Germany's Preussag (handing over control over Albania's chrome mines) against the competing bid of the U.S. led consortium of Macalloy Inc. in association with Rio Tinto Zimbabwe (RTZ).[26]

Large amounts of narco-dollars had also been recycled into the privatization programs leading to the acquisition of State assets by the mafias. In Albania, the privatization program had led virtually overnight to the development of a property-owning class firmly committed to the "free market". In Northern Albania, this class was associated with the Guegue "families" linked to the Democratic Party.

Controlled by the Democratic Party under the presidency of Sali Berisha (1992-97), Albania's largest financial "pyramid" VEFA Holdings had been set up by the Guegue "families" of Northern Albania with the support of Western banking interests. VEFA was under investigation in Italy in 1997 for its ties to the Mafia which allegedly used VEFA to launder large amounts of dirty money.[27]

According to one press report (based on intelligence sources), senior members of the Albanian government during the Presidency of Sali Berisha including cabinet members and members of the secret police SHIK were alleged to have been involved in drugs trafficking and illegal arms trading into Kosovo:

> The allegations are very serious. Drugs, arms, contraband cigarettes all are believed to have been handled by a company run openly by Albania's ruling Democratic Party, Shqiponja. ... In the course of 1996 Defense Minister, Safet Zhulali [was alleged] to had used his office to facilitate the transport of arms, oil and contraband cigarettes. ... Drugs barons from Kosovo operate in Albania with impunity, and much of the transportation of heroin and other drugs across Albania, from Macedonia and Greece en route to Italy, is believed to be organized by Shik, the state security police. ... Intelligence agents are convinced the chain of command in the rackets goes all the way to the top and have had no hesitation in naming ministers in their reports.[28]

The trade in narcotics and weapons was allowed to prosper despite the presence since 1993 of a large contingent of American troops at the Albanian-Macedonian border with a mandate to enforce the embargo. The West had turned a blind eye. The revenues from oil and narcotics were used to finance the purchase of arms (often in terms of direct barter): "Deliveries of oil to Macedonia (skirting the Greek embargo [in 1993-4] can be used to cover heroin, as do deliveries of Kalachnikov rifles to Albanian 'brothers' in Kosovo".[29]

The Northern tribal clans or "fares" had also developed links with Italy's crime syndicates.[30] In turn, the latter played a key role in smuggling arms across the Adriatic into the Albanian ports of Dures and Valona. At the outset in 1992, the weapons channelled into Kosovo were largely small arms including Kalashnikov AK-47 rifles, RPK and PPK machine-guns, 12.7 calibre heavy machine-guns, etc.

The proceeds of the narcotics trade had enabled the KLA to rapidly develop a force of some 30,000 men. The KLA had also acquired sophisticated weaponry including anti-aircraft and anti-armor rockets. According to Belgrade, some of the funds had come directly from the CIA "funneled through a so-called 'Government of Kosovo' based in Geneva, Switzerland. Its Washington office employs the public relations firm of Ruder Finn –notorious for its slanders of the Belgrade government".[31]

The KLA had also purchased electronic surveillance equipment which enabled it to receive NATO satellite information concerning the movement of the Yugoslav Army. The KLA training camp in Albania was said to "concentrate on heavy weapons training –rocket propelled grenades, medium caliber cannons, tanks and transporter use, as well as on communications, and command and control".[32]

These extensive deliveries of weapons to the Kosovo rebel army were consistent with Western geopolitical objectives. Not surprisingly, there was a "deafening silence" of the international media regarding the Kosovo arms-drugs trade. In the words of a 1994 Report of the Geopolitical Drug Watch:

> The trafficking [of drugs and arms] is basically being judged on its geostrategic implications. In Kosovo, drugs and weapons trafficking is fue ling geopolitical hopes and fears.[33]

The fate of Kosovo had already been carefully laid out prior to the signing of the 1995 Dayton agreement. NATO had entered an unwholesome "marriage of convenience" with the mafia. "Freedom fighters" were put in place, the narcotics trade enabled Washington and Bonn to "finance the Kosovo conflict" with the ultimate objective of destabilizing the Belgrade government and fully recolonizing the Balkans. The destruction of an entire country was the outcome.

Western governments which participated in the NATO operation bear a heavy burden of responsibility in the deaths of civilians, the impoverishment of both the ethnic Albanian and Serbian populations and the plight of those who were brutally uprooted from towns and villages in Kosovo as a result of the bombings.

NATO's Humanitarian Aftermath: The Mafia State

Supported by the United Nations, the U.S. State Department's project under Madeleine Albright was to spearhead a terrorist organization linked to Albanian and Italian crime syndicates, into the realm of civilian politics. The KLA was chosen by "the international community" to form a government integrated by known criminals. The Democratic Party of Kosovo (Partia Demokratike e Kosovës) headed by former KLA leader Hashim Thaci, also known as "The Snake", is essentially an outgrowth of the Kosovo Liberation Army (KLA).

In December 2010, following the "Assembly of Kosovo" elections in which Hashim Thaci's Democratic Party of Kosovo gained thirty-two percent of the vote, the Council of Europe released a report, claiming that Thaci and his "Kosovo Liberation Army" was a "mafia-like" organization involved in narcotics and arms trafficking and human organ trade. Hashim Thaci, before becoming "Prime Minister" of Kosovo was on the Interpol and FBI lists. The Kosovo Liberation Army (KLA) was known for its links to organized crime and the drug trade.

> The report, published by Dick Marty, a Swiss member of the Parliamentary Assembly of the Council of Europe (PACE), was a result of a two-year investigation into allegations first mentioned in the memoirs of former ICTY prosecutor Carla Del Ponte.[34]

The protégé of Madeleine Albright and Hillary Clinton is a known criminal.

Camp Bondsteel

Kosovo's mafia government headed by Prime Minister Hashim Thaci is a U.S. puppet regime, which takes its orders directly from Washington. Hosted by the Pristina regime, Kosovo is the home to one of America's largest military bases, Camp Bondsteel.

Bondsteel was built on contract to the Pentagon by Halliburton, through its (former) engineering subsidiary Kellogg, Brown and Root (KBR). Camp Bondsteel is considered to be "the largest and most expensive army base since Vietnam" with more than six thousand U.S. troops.

> Camp Bondsteel, the biggest "from scratch" foreign U.S. military base since the Vietnam War. ... It is located close to vital oil pipelines and energy corridors presently under construction, such as the U.S. sponsored Trans-Balkan oil pipeline. As a result, defense contractors–in particular Halliburton Oil subsidiary Brown & Root Services–are making a fortune.
>
> In June 1999, in the immediate aftermath of the bombing of Yugoslavia, U.S. forces seized 1,000 acres of farmland in southeast Kosovo at Urosevic, near the Macedonian border, and began the construction of a camp.
>
> Camp Bondsteel is known as the "grand dame" in a network of U.S. bases running both sides of the border between Kosovo and Macedonia. In less than three years it has been transformed from an encampment of tents to a self-sufficient, high-tech base-camp housing nearly seventy thousand troops–three quarters of all the U.S. troops stationed in Kosovo.
>
> There are twenty-five kilometers of roads and over three hundred buildings at Camp Bondsteel, surrounded by fourteen kilometers of earth and concrete barriers, eighty-four kilometers of concertina wire and eleven watchtowers. It is so big that it has downtown, midtown and uptown districts, retail outlets, twenty-four hour sports halls, a chapel, library and the best-equipped hospital anywhere in Europe. At present there are fifty-five Black Hawk and Apache helicopters based at Bondsteel and although it has no aircraft landing strip the location was chosen for its capacity to expand. There are suggestions that it could replace the U.S. air force base at Aviano in Italy.[35]

Camp Bondsteel was not the outgrowth of a humanitarian or "Just War" on behalf of Kosovar Albanians. The construction of

Camp Bondsteel had been envisaged well in advance of the bombings and invasion of Kosovo in 1999.

The plans to build Camp Bondsteel under a lucrative multi-billion dollar U.S. Department of Defense contract with Halliburton's Texas based subsidiary KBR were formulated while Dick Cheney was Halliburton's CEO.

Construction of Camp Bondsteel was initiated shortly after the 1999 invasion under the Clinton administration. Construction was completed during the Bush administration, after Dick Cheney had resigned his position as Halliburton's CEO:

The U.S. and NATO had advanced plans to bomb Yugoslavia before 1999, and many European political leaders now believe that the U.S. deliberately used the bombing of Yugoslavia to establish camp Bondsteel in Kosovo. According to Colonel Robert L. McCure, "Engineering planning for operations in Kosovo began months before the first bomb was dropped."[36]

One of the objectives underlying Camp Bondsteel was to protect the Albanian-Macedonian-Bulgarian Oil pipeline project (AMBO), which was to channel Caspian sea oil from the Bulgarian Black Sea port of Burgas to the Adriatic.

Coincidentally, two years prior to the invasion, in 1997, a senior executive of Brown & Root Energy, a subsidiary of Halliburton, Edward L. (Ted) Ferguson had been appointed to head AMBO. The feasibility plans for the AMBO pipeline were also undertaken by Halliburton's engineering company, Kellog, Brown & Root Ltd.

The AMBO agreement for the nine hundred seventeen kilometer long oil pipeline from Burgas to Valona, Albania, was signed in 2004.

Criminalization of the State

The establishment of a Kosovar mafia state sets an important precedent in international relations. We are not dealing with the familiar links of Western politicians to criminal syndicates. The relationship is far more sophisticated. The entire Kosovo state apparatus is criminalized.

Both the EU and the U.S. are using criminal organizations and criminalized political parties in Kosovo to reach their military and foreign policy goals. The latter in turn support the interests of the oil companies and defense contractors, not to mention the multi-billion dollar heroin trade out of Afghanistan.

At the institutional level, the U.S. administration, the EU, NATO and the UN are actively promoting the criminalization of the Kosovar State, which they control. In broad terms we are also dealing with the criminalization of U.S. foreign policy. These criminal organizations and parties were created to serve U.S. interests in Southern Europe.

For Washington, control over the Balkans constitutes the gateway to Eurasia. The 1999 invasion established a permanent U.S. military presence in Southern Europe, which serves the broader U.S. led war.

Notes

1. Roger Boyes and Eske Wright, Drugs Money Linked to the Kosovo Rebels, *The Times*, London, Monday, March 24, 1999.

2. *Ibid.*

3. Philip Smucker and Tim Butcher, "Shifting stance over KLA has 'betrayed' Albanians", *Daily Telegraph*, London, April 6, 1999.

4. KDOM Daily Report, released by the Bureau of European and Canadian Affairs, Office of South Central European Affairs, U.S. Department of State, Washington, DC, December 21, 1998; Compiled by EUR/SCE (202-647-4850) from daily reports of the U.S. element of the Kosovo Diplomatic Observer Mission, December 21, 1998.

5. "Rugova, sous protection serbe appelle a l'arret des raides", *Le Devoir*, Montreal, April 1, 1999.

6. See Alfred W. McCoy, *The Politics of Heroin in Southeast Asia*, Harper and Row, New York, 1972.

7. See John Dinges, *Our Man in Panama, The Shrewd Rise and Brutal Fall of Manuel Noriega*, Times Books, New York, 1991.

8. "The Dirtiest Bank of All" *Time*, July 29, 1991, p. 22.

9. Truth in Media, Phoenix, April 2, 1999; see also Michel Collon, *Poker Menteur*, Éditions EPO, Brussels, 1997.

10. Quoted in Truth in Media, Phoenix, April 2, 1999.

11. *Ibid*.

12. Geopolitical Drug Watch, No. 32, June 1994, p. 4.

13. Sean Gervasi, Germany, U.S. and the Yugoslav Crisis, *Covert Action Quarterly*, No. 43, Winter 1992-93.

14. See *Daily Telegraph*, December 29, 1993.

15. For further details see Michel Collon, *Poker Menteur*, Éditions EPO, Brussels, 1997, p 288.

16. Truth in Media, Kosovo in Crisis, Phoenix, April 2, 1999.

17. Deutsche Presse-Agentur, March 13, 1998.

18. *Ibid.*

19. *Daily News*, Ankara, March 5, 1997.

20. Quoted in Boyes and Wright, op cit.

21. ANA, Athens, January 28 ,1997, see also *Turkish Daily News*, January 29, 1997.

22. Brian Murphy, KLA Volunteers Lack Experience, The Associated Press, April 5, 1999.

23. *See Geopolitical Drug Watch*, No. 35, 1994, p. 3. See also Barry James, In Balkans, Arms for Drugs, *The International Herald Tribune* Paris, June 6, 1994.

24. *The Guardian*, March 25,1997.

25. For further details see Michel Chossudovsky, *La crisi albanese*, Edizioni Gruppo Abele, Torino, 1998.

26. *Ibid.*

27. Andrew Gumbel, The Gangster Regime We Fund, *The Independent*, February 14, 1997, p. 15.

28. *Ibid.*

29. Geopolitical Drug Watch, No. 35, 1994, p. 3.

30. Geopolitical Drug Watch, No. 66, p. 4.

31. Quoted in Workers' World, May 7, 1998.

32. See Government of Yugoslavia at http://www.gov.yu/terrorism/terrorist-camps.html.

33. Geopolitical Drug Watch, No 32, June 1994, p. 4.

34. Nebojsa Malic, Kosovo "Prime Minister" a Mobster Trafficking in Drugs, Body Parts, Global Research, December 27, 2010.

35. Paul Stuart, Camp Bondsteel and America's plans to control Caspian oil, WSWS.org, April 2002, http://www.wsws.org/articles/2002/apr2002/oil-a29.shtml.

36. Lenora Foerstel, Yugoslavia, Camp Bondsteel and the Caspian Sea, Global Research, January 30, 2008.

An earlier version of this chapter was written in April 1999 at the height of NATO's bombing campaign.

CHAPTER VII

U.S. Sponsored Coup d'Etat:
The Destabilization of Haiti

The armed insurrection which contributed to unseating President Aristide on February 29th 2004 was the result of a carefully staged military-intelligence operation, involving the U.S., France and Canada. The 2004 coup had set the stage for the installation of a U.S. puppet government in Port au Prince, which takes orders directly from Washington.

The Rebel paramilitary army crossed the border from the Dominican Republic in early February 2004. It constitutes a well armed, trained and equipped paramilitary unit integrated by former members of *Le Front pour l'avancement et le progrès d'Haiti* (FRAPH), the "plain clothes" death squadrons, involved in mass killings of civilians and political assassinations during the CIA sponsored 1991 military coup, which led to the overthrow of the democratically elected government of President Jean Bertrand Aristide.

The self-proclaimed *Front pour la Libération et la reconstruction nationale (FLRN)* (National Liberation and Reconstruction Front) was led by Guy Philippe, a former member of the Haitian Armed Forces and Police Chief. Philippe had been trained during the 1991 coup years by U.S. Special Forces in Ecuador, together with a dozen other Haitian Army officers.

The two other rebel commanders and associates of Guy Philippe, who led the attacks on Gonaives and Cap Haitien are Emmanuel Constant, nicknamed "Toto" and Jodel Chamblain, both of whom are former Tonton Macoute and leaders of FRAPH.

In 1994, Emmanuel Constant led the FRAPH assassination squadron into the village of Raboteau, in what was later identified as "The Raboteau massacre":

> One of the last of the infamous massacres happened in April 1994 in Raboteau, a seaside slum about 100 miles north of the capital. Raboteau has about 6,000 residents, most fish-

ermen and salt rakers, but it has a reputation as an opposition stronghold where political dissidents often went to hide… On April 18 [1994], 100 soldiers and about 30 paramilitaries arrived in Raboteau for what investigators would later call a "dress rehearsal." They rousted people from their homes, demanding to know where Amiot "Cubain" Metayer, a well-known Aristide supporter, was hiding. They beat people, inducing a pregnant woman to miscarry, and forced others to drink from open sewers. Soldiers tortured a 65-year-old blind man until he vomited blood. He died the next day.

The soldiers returned before dawn on April 22. They ransacked homes and shot people in the streets, and when the residents fled for the water, other soldiers fired at them from boats they had commandeered. Bodies washed ashore for days; some were never found. The number of victims ranges from two dozen to 30. Hundreds more fled the town, fearing further reprisals.[1]

During the military government (1991-1994), FRAPH was (unofficially) under the jurisdiction of the Armed Forces, taking orders from Commander in Chief General Raoul Cedras. According to a 1996 UN Human Rights Commission report, FRAPH had been supported by the CIA.

Under the military dictatorship, the narcotics trade, was protected by the military Junta, which in turn was supported by the CIA. The 1991 coup leaders including the FRAPH paramilitary commanders were on the CIA payroll.[2] Emmanuel Constant alias "Toto" confirmed in a CBS "60 Minutes" in 1995, that the CIA paid him about $700 a month and that he created FRAPH, while on the CIA payroll.[3] According to Constant, the FRAPH had been formed "with encouragement and financial backing from the U.S. Defense Intelligence Agency and the CIA."[4]

The Civilian "Opposition"

The so-called *"Democratic Convergence" (DC)* was a group of some 200 political organizations, led by former Port-au-Prince mayor Evans Paul. The "Democratic Convergence" (DC) together with *"The Group of 184 Civil Society Organizations" (G-184)* had formed a so-called "*Democratic Platform of Civil Society Organizations and Opposition Political Parties*".

The Group of 184 (G-184), was headed by André (Andy) Apaid, a U.S. citizen of Haitian parents, born in the U.S..[5] Andy Apaid owns Alpha Industries, one of Haiti's largest cheap labor export assembly lines established during the Duvalier era. His sweatshop factories produce textile products and assemble electronic products for a number of U.S. firms including Sperry/Unisys, IBM, Remington and Honeywell. Apaid is the largest industrial employer in Haiti with a workforce of some 4000 workers. Wages paid in Andy Apaid's factories are as low as 68 cents a day.[6] The current minimum wage is of the order of $1.50 a day:

> The U.S.-based National Labor Committee, which first revealed the Kathie Lee Gifford sweat shop scandal, reported several years ago that Apaid's factories in Haiti's free trade zone often pay below the minimum wage and that his employees are forced to work 78-hour weeks.[7]

Apaid was a firm supporter of the 1991 military coup. Both the *Convergence démocratique* and the G-184 have links to the FLRN (former FRAPH death squadrons) headed by Guy Philippe. The FLRN is also known to receive funding from the Haitian business community.

In other words, there was no watertight division between the civilian opposition, which claims to be non-violent and the FLRN paramilitary. The FLRN was collaborating with the so-called "Democratic Platform."

The Role of the National Endowment for Democracy (NED)

In Haiti, this "civil society opposition" was bankrolled by the National Endowment for Democracy which works hand in glove with the CIA. The Democratic Platform was supported by the International Republican Institute (IRI) , which is an arm of the National Endowment for Democracy (NED). Senator John McCain is Chairman of IRI's Board of Directors.[8]

G-184 leader Andy Apaid was in liaison with Secretary of State Colin Powell in the days prior to the kidnapping and deportation of President Aristide by U.S. forces on February 29, 2004. His umbrella organization of elite business organizations and religious NGOs, which is also supported by the International Republican Institute (IRI), receives sizeable amounts of money from the European Union.[9]

It is worth recalling that the NED, (which overseas the IRI) although not formally part of the CIA, performs an important intelligence function within the arena of civilian political parties and NGOs. It was created in 1983, when the CIA was being accused of covertly bribing politicians and setting up phony civil society front organizations. According to Allen Weinstein, who was responsible for setting up the NED during the Reagan Administration: "A lot of what we do today was done covertly 25 years ago by the CIA."[10]

The NED channels congressional funds to the four institutes: The International Republican Institute (IRI), the National Democratic Institute for International Affairs (NDI), the Center for International Private Enterprise (CIPE), and the American Center for International Labor Solidarity (ACILS). These organizations are said to be "uniquely qualified to provide technical assistance to aspiring democrats worldwide."[11]

In other words, there is a division of tasks between the CIA and the NED. While the CIA provides covert support to armed paramilitary rebel groups and death squadrons, the NED and its four constituent organizations finance "civilian" political parties and non governmental organizations with a view to instating American "democracy" around the World.

The NED constitutes, so to speak, the CIA's "civilian arm". CIA-NED interventions in different part of the World are characterized by a consistent pattern, which is applied in numerous countries.

The NED provided funds to the "civil society" organizations in Venezuela, which initiated an attempted coup against President Hugo Chavez. In Venezuela it was the "Democratic Coordination", which was the recipient of NED support; in Haiti it is the "Democratic Convergence" and G-184.

Similarly, in former Yugoslavia, the CIA channeled support to the Kosovo Liberation Army (KLA) (since 1995), a paramilitary group involved in terrorist attacks on the Yugoslav police and military (See Chapter VI). Meanwhile, the NED through the "Center for International Private Enterprise" (CIPE) was backing the Democratic Opposition of Serbia (DOS) coalition in Serbia and Montenegro. More specifically, NED was financing the G-17, an opposition group of economists responsible for formulating (in liaison with the IMF) the DOS coalition's "free market" reform platform in the 2000 presidential election, which led to the downfall of Slobodan Milosevic.

The IMF's Bitter "Economic Medicine"

The IMF and the World Bank are key players in the process of economic and political destabilization. While carried out under the auspices of an intergovernmental body, the IMF reforms tend to support U.S. strategic and foreign policy objectives.

Based on the so-called "Washington consensus", IMF austerity and restructuring measures through their devastating impacts, often contribute to triggering social and ethnic strife. IMF reforms have often precipitated the downfall of elected governments. In extreme cases of economic and social dislocation, the IMF's bitter economic medicine has contributed to the destabilization of entire countries, as occurred in Somalia, Rwanda and Yugoslavia.[12]

The IMF program is a consistent instrument of economic dislocation. The IMF's reforms contribute to reshaping and downsizing State institutions through drastic austerity measures. The latter are implemented alongside other forms of intervention and political interference, including CIA covert activities in support of rebel paramilitary groups and opposition political parties.

Moreover, so-called "Emergency Recovery" and "Post-conflict" reforms are often introduced under IMF guidance, in the wake of a civil war, a regime change or "a national emergency".

In Haiti, the IMF sponsored "free market" reforms have been carried out consistently since the Duvalier era. They have been applied in several stages since the first election of president Aristide in 1990.

The 1991 military coup, which took place 8 months following Jean Bertrand Aristide's accession to the presidency, was in part intended to reverse the Aristide government's progressive reforms and reinstate the neoliberal policy agenda of the Duvalier era.

A former World Bank official Mr. Marc Bazin was appointed Prime minister by the Military Junta in June 1992. In fact, it was the U.S. State Department which sought his appointment.

Bazin had a track record of working for the "Washington consensus." In 1983, he had been appointed Finance Minister under the Duvalier regime, In fact he had been recommended to the Finance portfolio by the IMF: "President-for-Life Jean-Claude Duvalier had agreed to the appointment of an IMF nominee, former World Bank official Marc Bazin, as Minister of Finance".[13] Bazin, who was considered Washington's "favorite", later ran against Aristide in the 1990 presidential elections.

Bazin, was called in by the Military Junta in 1992 to form a so-called "consensus government". It is worth noting that it was precisely during Bazin's term in office as Prime Minister that the political massacres and extra judicial killings by the CIA supported FRAPH death squadrons were unleashed, leading to the killing of more than 4000 civilians. Some 300,000 people became internal refugees, "thousands more fled across the border to the Dominican Republic, and more than 60,000 took to the high seas" (Statement of Dina Paul Parks, Executive Director, National Coalition for Haitian Rights, Committee on Senate Judiciary, U.S. Senate, Washington DC, October 2002). Meanwhile, the CIA had launched a smear campaign representing Aristide as "mentally unstable"[14]

The 1994 U.S. Military Intervention

Following three years of military rule, the U.S. intervened in 1994, sending in 20,000 occupation troops and "peace-keepers" to Haiti. The U.S. military intervention was not intended to restore democracy. Quite the contrary: it was carried out to prevent a popular insurrection against the military Junta and its neoliberal cohorts.

In other words, the U.S. military occupation was implemented to ensure political continuity.

While the members of the military Junta were sent into exile, the return to constitutional government required compliance to IMF diktats, thereby foreclosing the possibility of a progressive "alternative" to the neoliberal agenda. Moreover, U.S. troops remained in the country until 1999. The Haitian armed forces were disbanded and the U.S. State Department hired a mercenary company DynCorp to provide "technical advice" in restructuring the Haitian National Police (HNP).

"DynCorp has always functioned as a cut-out for Pentagon and CIA covert operations."[15] Under DynCorp advice in Haiti, former Tonton Macoute and Haitian military officers involved in the 1991 Coup d'Etat were brought into the HNP.[16]

In October 1994, Aristide returned from exile and reintegrated the presidency until the end of his mandate in 1996. "Free market" reformers were brought into his Cabinet. A new wave of deadly macroeconomic policies was adopted under a so-called Emergency Economic Recovery Plan (EERP) "that sought to achieve rapid macroeconomic stabilization, restore public administration, and attend to the most pressing needs."[17]

The restoration of Constitutional government had been negotiated behind closed doors with Haiti's external creditors. Prior to Aristide's reinstatement as the country's president, the new government was obliged to clear the country's debt arrears with its external creditors. In fact the new loans provided by the World Bank, the Inter-American Development Bank (IDB), and the IMF were used to meet Haiti's obligations with international creditors. Fresh money was used to pay back old debt leading to a spiraling external debt.

Broadly coinciding with the military government, Gross Domestic Product (GDP) declined by 30 percent (1992-1994). With a per capita income of $250 per annum (2003), Haiti is the poorest country in the Western hemisphere and among the poorest in the world.[18] The World Bank estimated unemployment to be of the order of 60 percent.

In the wake of three years of military rule and economic decline, there was no "Economic Emergency Recovery" as envisaged under the IMF loan agreement. In fact quite the opposite: The IMF imposed "stabilization" under the "Recovery" program required further budget cuts in almost non-existent social sector programs. A civil service reform program was launched, which consisted in reducing the size of the civil service and the firing of "surplus" State employees. The IMF-World Bank package was in part instrumental in the paralysis of public services, leading to the eventual demise of the entire State system. In a country where health and educational services were virtually nonexistent, the IMF had demanded the lay off of "surplus" teachers and health workers with a view to meeting its target for the budget deficit.

Washington's foreign policy initiatives were coordinated with the application of the IMF's deadly economic medicine. The country had been literally pushed to the brink of economic and social disaster.

The Fate of Haitian Agriculture

More than 75 percent of the Haitian population is engaged in agriculture, producing both food crops for the domestic market as well a number of cash crops for export. Already during the Duvalier era, the peasant economy had been undermined. With the adoption of the IMF-World Bank sponsored trade reforms, the agricultural system, which previously produced food for the local market, had been destabilized. With the lifting of trade barriers, the local market was opened up to the dumping of U.S. agricultural surpluses including rice, sugar and corn, leading to the destruction of the entire peasant economy. Gonaives, which used to be Haiti's rice basket region, with extensive paddy fields had been precipitated into bankruptcy:

> By the end of the 1990s Haiti's local rice production had been reduced by half and rice imports from the U.S. accounted for over half of local rice sales. The local farming population was devastated, and the price of rice rose drastically [19]

In a matter of a few years, Haiti, a small impoverished country in the Caribbean, had become the World's fourth largest importer of American rice after Japan, Mexico and Canada.

The Second Wave of IMF Reforms

The presidential elections were scheduled for November 23, 2000. The Clinton Administration had put an embargo on development aid to Haiti in 2000. Barely two weeks prior to the elections, the outgoing administration signed a Letter of Intent with the IMF. Perfect timing: the agreement with the IMF virtually foreclosed from the outset any departure from the neoliberal agenda.

The Minister of Finance had sent the amended budget to the Parliament on December 14th. Donor support was conditional upon its rubber stamp approval by the Legislature. While Aristide had promised to increase the minimum wage, embark on school construction and literacy programs, the hands of the new government were tied. All major decisions regarding the State budget, the management of the public sector, public investment, privatization, trade and monetary policy had already been taken. They were part of the agreement reached with the IMF in November 2000.

In 2003, the IMF imposed the application of a so-called "flexible price system in fuel", which immediately triggered an inflationary spiral. The currency was devalued. Petroleum prices increased by about 130 percent in January-February 2003, which served to increase popular resentment against the Aristide government, which had supported the implementation of the IMF economic reforms.

The hike in fuel prices contributed to a 40 percent increase in consumer prices (CPI) in 2002-2003.[20] In turn, the IMF had demanded, despite the dramatic increase in the cost of living, a freeze on wages as a means to "controlling inflationary pressures." The IMF had in fact pressured the government to lower public sector salaries (including those paid to teachers and health workers). The IMF had also demanded the phasing out of the statutory minimum wage of approximately 25 cents an hour. "Labour market flexibility", meaning wages paid below the statutory minimum wage would, according to the IMF, contribute to attracting foreign investors. The daily minimum wage was $3.00 in 1994, declining to about $1.50- 1.75 (depending on the gourde-dollar exchange rate) in 2004.

In an utterly twisted logic, Haiti's abysmally low wages, which had been part of the IMF-World Bank "cheap labor" policy framework since the 1980s, were viewed as a means to improving the standard of living. In other words, sweatshop conditions in the assembly industries (in a totally unregulated labor market) and forced labor conditions in Haiti's agricultural plantations are considered by the IMF as a key to achieving economic prosperity, because they "attract foreign investment."

The country was in the straightjacket of a spiraling external debt. In a bitter irony, the IMF-World Bank sponsored austerity measures in the social sectors were imposed in a country which had 1,2 medical doctors for 10,000 inhabitants and where the large majority of the population is illiterate. State social services, which were virtually nonexistent during the Duvalier period, have collapsed.

The result of IMF ministrations was a further collapse in purchasing power, which had also affected middle income groups. Meanwhile, interest rates had skyrocketed. In the Northern and Eastern parts of the country, the hikes in fuel prices had led to a virtual paralysis of transportation and public services including water and electricity.

While a humanitarian catastrophe was looming, the collapse of the economy spearheaded by the IMF, had served to boost the popularity of the Democratic Platform, which had accused Aristide of "economic mismanagement." Needless to say, the leaders of the Democratic Platform including Andy Apaid –who actually owns the sweatshops– are the main protagonists of the low wage economy.

Applying the Kosovo Model

In February 2003, Washington announced the appointment of James B. Foley as Ambassador to Haiti. Foley had been a State Department spokesman under the Clinton administration during the war on Kosovo. He previously held a position at NATO headquarters in Brussels. Foley had been sent to Port-au-Prince in advance of the CIA sponsored operation. He was transferred to Port-au-Prince in September 2003, from a prestige diplomatic position in Geneva, where he was Deputy Head of Mission to the UN European office.

It is worth recalling Ambassador Foley's involvement in support of the Kosovo Liberation Army (KLA) in 1999. (See Chapter VI)

Amply documented, the Kosovo Liberation Army (KLA) was financed by drug money and supported by the CIA. The KLA had been involved in similar targeted political assassinations and killings of civilians, in the months leading up to the 1999 NATO invasion as well as in its aftermath. Following the NATO led invasion and occupation of Kosovo, the KLA was transformed into the Kosovo Protection Force (KPF) under UN auspices. Rather than being disarmed to prevent the massacres of civilians, a terrorist organization with links to organized crime and the Balkans drug trade, was granted a legitimate political status.

At the time of the Kosovo war, the ambassador to Haiti James Foley was in charge of State Department briefings, working closely with his NATO counterpart in Brussels, Jamie Shea. Barely two months before the onslaught of the NATO led war on 24 March 1999, James Foley had called for the "transformation" of the KLA into a respectable political organization:

> We want to develop a good relationship with them [the KLA] as they transform themselves into a politically-oriented organization ... [W]e believe that we have a lot of advice and a lot of help that we can provide to them if they become precisely the kind of political actor we would like to see them become. ... If we can help them and they want us to help them in that effort of transformation, I think it's nothing that anybody can argue with.[21]

In the wake of the invasion "a self-proclaimed Kosovar administration was set up composed of the KLA and the Democratic Union Movement (LBD), a coalition of five opposition parties opposed to Rugova's Democratic League (LDK). In addition to the position of prime minister, the KLA controlled the ministries of finance, public order and defense."[22]

The U.S. State Department's position as conveyed in Foley's statement was that the KLA would "not be allowed to continue as a military force but would have the chance to move forward in their quest for self government under a 'different context'" meaning the inauguration of a de facto "narco-democracy" under NATO protection.[23]

With regard to the drug trade, Kosovo and Albania occupy a similar position to that of Haiti: they constitute "a hub" in the transit (transshipment) of narcotics from the Golden Crescent, through Iran and Turkey into Western Europe. While supported by the CIA, Germany's *Bundes Nachrichten Dienst* (BND) and NATO, the KLA has links to the Albanian Mafia and criminal syndicates involved in the narcotics trade (See Chapter VI).

Is this the model for Haiti, as formulated in 1999 by the U.S. Ambassador to Haiti James Foley?

For the CIA and the State Department the FLRN and *Guy Philippe* are to Haiti what the KLA and Hashim Thaci are to Kosovo.

In other words, Washington's design is "regime change": topple the Lavalas administration and install a compliant U.S. puppet regime, integrated by the Democratic Platform and the self-proclaimed *Front pour la libération et la reconstruction nationale* (FLRN), whose leaders are former FRAPH and Tonton Macoute terrorists. The latter were slated to integrate a "national unity government" alongside the leaders of the Democratic Convergence and The Group of 184 Civil Society Organizations led by Andy Apaid. More specifically, the FLRN led by Guy Philippe is slated to rebuild the Haitian Armed forces, which were disbanded in 1995.

What is at stake is an eventual power sharing arrangement between the various Opposition groups and the CIA supported Rebels, which have links to the cocaine transit trade from Colombia via Haiti to Florida. The protection of this trade has a bearing on the formation of a new "narco-government", which will serve U.S. interests.

A bogus (symbolic) disarmament of the rebels may be contemplated under international supervision, as occurred with the KLA in Kosovo in 2000. The "former terrorists" could then be integrated into the civilian police as well as into the task of "rebuilding" the Haitian Armed forces under U.S. supervision.

What this scenario suggests, is that the Duvalier-era terrorist structures have been restored. A program of civilian killings and political assassinations directed against Lavalas supporters is in fact already underway.

In other words, if Washington were really motivated by humanitarian considerations, why then was it supporting and financing the FRAPH death squadrons? Its objective is not to prevent the massacre of civilians. Modelled on previous CIA led operations (e.g. Guatemala, Indonesia, El Salvador), the FLRN death squadrons had been set loose and are involved in targeted political assassinations of Aristide supporters.

The Narcotics Transshipment Trade

While the real economy had been driven into bankruptcy under the brunt of the IMF reforms, the narcotics transshipment trade continued to flourish. According to the U.S. Drug Enforcement Administration (DEA), Haiti remains "the major drug trans-shipment country for the entire Caribbean region, funneling huge shipments of cocaine from Colombia to the United States."[24]

It is estimated that Haiti is now responsible for 14 percent of all the cocaine entering the United States, representing billions of dollars of revenue for organized crime and U.S. financial institutions, which launder vast amounts of dirty money. The global trade in narcotics is estimated to be of the order of 500 billion dollars.

Much of this transshipment trade goes directly to Miami, which also constitutes a haven for the recycling of dirty money into bona fide investments, e.g. in real estate and other related activities.

The evidence confirms that the CIA was protecting this trade during the Duvalier era as well as during the military dictatorship (1991-1994). In 1987, Senator John Kerry as Chairman of the Subcommittee on Narcotics, Terrorism and International Operations of the Senate Foreign Affairs Committee was entrusted with a major investigation, which focused on the links between the CIA and the drug trade, including the laundering of drug money to finance armed insurgencies. "The Kerry Report" published in 1989, while centering its attention on the financing of the Nicaraguan Contra, also included a section on Haiti:

> Kerry had developed detailed information on drug trafficking by Haiti's military rulers that led to the indictment in Miami in 1988, of Lt. Col. Jean Paul. The indictment was a major embarrassment to the Haitian military, especially since Paul defiantly refused to surrender to U.S. authorities.. In November 1989, Col. Paul was found dead after he consumed a traditional Haitian good will gift –a bowel of pumpkin soup. ...
>
> The U.S. senate also heard testimony in 1988 that then interior minister, Gen. Williams Regala, and his DEA liaison officer, protected and supervised cocaine shipments. The testimony also charged the then Haitian military commander Gen. Henry Namphy with accepting bribes from Colombian traffickers in return for landing rights in the mid 1980's.
>
> It was in 1989 that yet another military coup brought Lt. Gen. Prosper Avril to power. ... According to a witness before Senator John Kerry's subcommittee, Avril is in fact a major player in Haiti's role as a transit point in the cocaine trade.[25]

Jack Blum, who was Kerry's Special Counsel, points to the complicity of U.S. officials in a 1996 statement to the U.S. Senate Select Committee on Intelligence on Drug Trafficking and the Contra War:

> In Haiti … intelligence "sources" of ours in the Haitian military had turned their facilities over to the drug cartels. Instead of putting pressure on the rotten leadership of the military, we defended them. We held our noses and looked the other way as they and their criminal friends in the United States distributed cocaine in Miami, Philadelphia and New, York.[26]

Haiti not only remains at the hub of the transshipment cocaine trade, the latter has grown markedly since the 1980s. The current crisis bears a relationship to Haiti's role in the drug trade. Washington wants a compliant Haitian government which will protect the drug transshipment routes, out of Colombia through Haiti and into Florida.

The inflow of narco-dollars –which remains the major source of the country's foreign exchange earnings– are used to service Haiti's spiraling external debt, thereby also serving the interests of the external creditors.

In this regard, the liberalization of the foreign-exchange market imposed by the IMF has provided (despite the authorities pro forma commitment to combating the drug trade) a convenient avenue for the laundering of narco-dollars in the domestic banking system. The inflow of narco-dollars alongside bona fide "remittances" from Haitians living abroad, are deposited in the commercial banking system and exchanged into local currency. The foreign exchange proceeds of these inflows can then be recycled towards the Treasury where they are used to meet debt servicing obligations.

Haiti, however, reaps a very small percentage of the total foreign exchange proceeds of this lucrative contraband. Most of the revenue resulting from the cocaine transshipment trade accrues to criminal intermediaries in the wholesale and retail narcotics trade, to the intelligence agencies which protect the drug trade as well as to the financial and banking institutions where the proceeds of this criminal activity are laundered.

The narco-dollars are also channeled into "private banking" accounts in numerous offshore banking havens. (These havens are controlled by the large Western banks and financial institutions). Drug money is also invested in a number of financial instruments including hedge funds and stock market transactions. The major Wall Street and European banks and stock brokerage firms launder billions of dollars resulting from the trade in narcotics.

Moreover, the expansion of the dollar denominated money supply by the Federal Reserve System, including the printing of billions of dollars of U.S. dollar notes for the purposes of narco-transactions constitutes profit for the Federal Reserve and its constituent private banking institutions of which the most important is the New York Federal Reserve Bank.[27]

In other words, the Wall Street financial establishment, which plays a behind the scenes role in the formulation of U.S. foreign policy, has a vested interest in retaining the Haiti transshipment trade, while installing a reliable "narco-democracy" in Port-au-Prince, which will effectively protect the transshipment routes.

It should be noted that since the advent of the Euro as a global currency, a significant share of the narcotics trade is now conducted in Euro rather than U.S. dollars. In other words, the Euro and the dollar are competing narco-currencies.

The Latin American cocaine trade –including the transshipment trade through Haiti– is largely conducted in U.S. dollars. This shift out of dollar denominated narco-transactions, which undermines the hegemony of the U.S. dollar as a global currency, largely pertains to the Middle East, Central Asian and the Southern European drug routes.

Media Manipulation

In the weeks leading up to the February 2004 Coup d'Etat, the media largely focused its attention on the pro-Aristide "armed gangs" and "thugs", without providing an understanding of the role of the FLRN Rebels.

Deafening silence: not a word was mentioned in official statements and UN resolutions regarding the nature of the FLRN. This should come as no surprise: the U.S. Ambassador to the UN (the man who sits on the UN Security Council) John Negroponte played a key role in the CIA supported Honduran death squadrons in the 1980s when he was U.S. ambassador to Honduras.[28]

The FLRN rebels are extremely well equipped and trained forces. The Haitian people know who they are. They are Tonton Macoute of the Duvalier era and former FRAPH assassins.

The Western media is mute on the issue, blaming the violence on President Aristide. When it acknowledges that the Liberation Army is composed of death squadrons, it fails to examine the broader implications of its statements and that these death squadrons are a creation of the CIA and the Defense Intelligence Agency.

The *New York Times* has acknowledged that the "non violent" civil society opposition is in fact collaborating with the death squadrons, "accused of killing thousands", but all this is described as "accidental". No historical understanding is provided. Who are these death squadron leaders? All we are told is that they have established an "alliance" with the "non-violent" good guys who belong to the "political opposition". And it is all for a good and worthy cause, which is to remove the elected president and "restore democracy":

> As Haiti's crisis lurches toward civil war, a tangled web of alliances, some of them accidental, has emerged. It has linked the interests of a political opposition movement that has embraced nonviolence to a group of insurgents that includes a former leader of death squads accused of killing thousands, a former police chief accused of plotting a coup and a ruthless gang once aligned with Mr. Aristide that has now turned against him. Given their varied origins, those arrayed against Mr. Aristide are hardly unified, though they all share an ardent wish to see him removed from power.[29]

There is nothing spontaneous or "accidental" in the rebel attacks or in the "alliance" between the leader of the death squadrons Guy Philippe and Andy Apaid, owner of the largest industrial sweatshop in Haiti and leader of the G-184.

The armed rebellion was part of a carefully planned military-intelligence operation. The Armed Forces of the Dominican Republic had detected guerilla training camps inside the Dominican Republic on the Northeast Haitian-Dominican border.[30]

Both the armed rebels and their civilian "non-violent" counter-parts were involved in the plot to unseat the president. G-184 leader Andre Apaid was in touch with Colin Powell in the weeks leading up to the overthrow of Aristide; Guy Philippe and "Toto" Emmanuel Constant have links to the CIA; there are indications that Rebel Commander Guy Philippe and the political leader of the *Revolutionary Artibonite Resistance Front* Winter Etienne were in liaison with U.S. officials.[31]

While the U.S. had repeatedly stated that it will uphold Constitutional government, the replacement of Aristide by a more compliant individual had always been part of the Bush Administration's agenda.

On February 20, 2004, nine days before the coup d'État, U.S. Ambassador James Foley called in a team of four military experts from the U.S. Southern Command, based in Miami. Officially their mandate was "to assess threats to the embassy and its personnel."[32] U.S. Special Forces are already in the country. Washington had announced that three U.S. naval vessels "have been put on standby to go to Haiti as a precautionary measure". The Saipan is equipped with Vertical takeoff Harrier fighters and attack helicopters. The other two vessels are the Oak Hill and Trenton. Some 2,200 U.S. Marines from the 24th Marine Expeditionary Unit, at Camp Lejeune, N.C. could be deployed to Haiti at short notice, according to Washington.

With the departure of President Aristide, Washington, however, has no intention of disarming its proxy rebel paramilitary army, which is now slated to play a role in the "transition". In other words, the Bush administration will not act to prevent the occurrence of killings and political assassinations of Lavalas and Aristide supporters in the wake of the president's kidnapping and deportation.

Needless to say, the Western media has not in the least analyzed the historical background of the Haitian crisis. The role played by the CIA has not been mentioned. The so-called "international community", which claims to be committed to governance and democracy, has turned a blind eye to the killings of civilians by a U.S. sponsored paramilitary army. The "rebel leaders", who were commanders in the FRAPH death squads in the 1990s, are now being upheld by the U.S. media as bona fide opposition spokesmen. Meanwhile, the legitimacy of the former elected president is questioned because he is said to be responsible for "a worsening economic and social situation."

The worsening economic and social situation is largely attributable to the devastating economic reforms imposed by the IMF since the 1980s. The restoration of Constitutional government in 1994 was conditional upon the acceptance of the IMF's deadly economic therapy, which in turn foreclosed the possibility of a meaningful democracy. High ranking government officials respectively within the Andre Preval and Jean Bertrand Aristide governments were indeed compliant with IMF diktats. Despite this compliance, Aristide had been "blacklisted" and demonized by Washington.

The Militarization of the Caribbean Basin

Washington seeks to reinstate Haiti as a full-fledged U.S. colony, with all the appearances of a functioning democracy. The objective is to impose a puppet regime in Port-au-Prince and establish a permanent U.S. military presence in Haiti.

The U.S. Administration ultimately seeks to militarize the Caribbean basin.

The island of Hispaniola is a gateway to the Caribbean basin, strategically located between Cuba to the North West and Venezuela to the South. The militarization of the island, with the establishment of U.S. military bases, is not only intended to put political pressure on Cuba and Venezuela, it is also geared towards the protection of the multibillion dollar narcotics transshipment trade through Haiti, from production sites in Colombia, Peru and Bolivia.

The militarization of the Caribbean basin is, in some regards, similar to that imposed by Washington on the Andean Region of South America under "Plan Colombia", renamed "The Andean Initiative". The latter constitutes the basis for the militarisation of oil and gas wells, as well as pipeline routes and transportation corridors. It also protects the narcotics trade.

Notes

1. *St Petersburg Times*, Florida, September 1, 2002.
2. See Paul DeRienzo, Haiti's Nightmare: The Cocaine Coup and the CIA Connection, http://globalresearch.ca/articles/RIE402A.html , Global Research, February 25, 20014. See also see Jim Lobe, IPS, October 11, 1996.
3. See *Miami Herald*, August 1, 2001.
4. *Miami New Times*, February 26, 2004.
5. *Haiti Progres*, http://www.haiti-progres.com/eng11-12.html.
6. *Miami Times*, February 26, 2004.
7. *Daily News*, New York, February 24, 2004.
8. See Laura Flynn, Pierre Labossière and Robert Roth, Hidden from the Headlines: The U.S. War Against Haiti, California-based Haiti Action Committee (HAC), http://www.haitiprogres.com/eng11-12.html.
9. http://haitisupport.gn.apc.org/184%20EC.htm.
10. *Washington Post*, September 21, 1991.
11. See IRI, http://www.iri.org/history.asp.
12. See Michel Chossudovsky, *The Globalization of Poverty and the New World Order,* Second Edition, 2003, http://globalresearch.ca/globaloutlook/GofP.html.
13. *Mining Annual Review*, June, 1983.
14. *Boston Globe*, September 21, 1994.
15. See Jeffrey St. Clair and Alexander Cockburn, Counterpunch, February 27, 2002, http://www.corpwatch.org/issues/PID.jsp?articleid=1988.
16. See Ken Silverstein, Privatizing War, *The Nation*, July 28, 1997, http://www.mtholyoke.edu/acad/intrel/silver.htm.
17. See IMF Approves Three-Year ESAF Loan for Haiti, Washington, 1996, http://www.imf.org/external/np/sec/pr/1996/pr9653.htm.
18. See World Bank, Haiti: The Challenges of Poverty Reduction, Washington, August 1998, http://lnweb18.worldbank.org/External/lac/lac.nsf/0/8479e9126e35 37f0852567ea000fa239/$FILE/Haiti1.doc.
19. See Rob Lyon, Haiti-There is no solution under Capitalism! Socialist Appeal. February 24, 2004, http://cleveland.indymedia.org/news/2004/02/9095.php.
20. See Haiti–Letter of Intent, Memorandum of Economic and Financial Policies, and Technical Memorandum of Understanding, Port-au-Prince, Haiti June 10, 2003, http://www.imf.org/external/np/loi/2003/hti/01/index.htm.
21. Quoted in The *New York Times*, February 2, 1999.
22. Michel Chossudovsky, NATO's War of Aggression against Yugoslavia, Global Research, 1999, http://www.globalresearch.ca/articles/CHO309C.html.
23. *Ibid.*
24. See U.S. House of Representatives, Criminal Justice, Drug Policy and Human Resources Subcommittee, FDHC Transcripts, April 12, 2000.
25. Paul DeRienzo, Haiti's Nightmare: The Cocaine Coup & The CIA Connection, *The Shadow*, Spring 1994.
26. http://www.totse.com/en/politics/central_intelligence_agency/ciacont2.html.

27. Jeffrey Steinberg, Dope, Inc. Is $600 Billion and Growing, Executive Intelligence Review, December 14, 2001, http://www.larouchepub.com/other/2001/284 8dope_money.html.
28. See *San Francisco Examiner*, October 20, 2001
http://www.flora.org/mai/forum/31397.
29 *New York Times*, February 26, 2004.
30. El ejército dominicano informó a Aristide sobre los entrenamientos rebeldes en la frontera, El Caribe, February 27, 2004, http://www.elcaribe.com.do/articulo_multimedios.aspx?id=2645&guid=AB38144D39B24C6FBA4213AC40DD3 A01&Seccion=64).
31. See BBC, February 27, 2004,
http://news.bbc.co.uk/2/hi/americas/3496690.stm.
32. *Seattle Times*, February 20, 2004.

The above text was written in the last days of February 2004 in response to the barrage of disinformation in the mainstream media. It was completed on February 29, the day of President Jean Bertrand Aristide's kidnapping and deportation by U.S. Forces.

The armed insurrection which contributed to unseating President Aristide on February 29, 2004 was the result of a carefully staged military-intelligence operation, involving the U.S., France and Canada. The 2004 coup had set the stage for the installation of a U.S. puppet government in Port-au-Prince, which takes orders directly from Washington.

Minor editorial corrections were made to the original draft since its publication on February 29, 2004.

Chapter VIII
"Operation Libya" and the Battle for Oil Redrawing the Map of Africa

The 2011 U.S.-NATO led war on Libya was a multi-trillion dollar trophy for the United States.

Libya's oil reserves are twice those of the United States.

The U.S.-NATO intervention was also intent upon excluding China from the broader region and edging out China's National Petroleum Corp (CNPC), which was a major player in Libya.

Libya is the gateway to the Sahel and Central Africa. More generally, what is at stake is the redrawing of the map of Africa at the expense of France's historical spheres of influence, namely a process of neocolonial redivision.

The geopolitical and economic implications of a U.S.-NATO led military intervention directed against Libya are far-reaching.

Libya is among the World's largest oil economies with approximately 3.5% of global oil reserves.

Al Qaeda Rebels and NATO Join Hands

The conquest of Libya's oil wealth was implemented with the support of America's "pro-democracy" Al Qaeda paramilitary brigades. The "Liberation" of Tripoli was carried out by "former" members of the Libya Islamic Fighting Group (LIFG) under the supervision of NATO Special Forces.

Concepts are turned upside down: The U.S.-NATO military alliance is supporting a rebellion integrated by Islamic terrorists, in the name of the "War on Terrorism". Barely acknowledged by the Western media, *Al-Jamaa al-Islamiyyah al-Muqatilah bi Liby*a, the Libya Islamic Fighting Group (LIFG) was an integral part of the Libyan "Opposition".

The Libya Islamic Fighting Group (LIFG), aligned with Al Qaeda, was in the frontline of the U.S.-NATO armed insurrection. The jihadists and NATO worked hand in glove. These "former" Al Qaeda affiliated brigades constitute the backbone of the "pro-democracy" rebellion, which in a bitter irony was also supported by prominent "progressives" as well as segments of the U.S. "alternative media".

Special forces composed of U.S. Navy SEALS, British Special SAS Forces and French legionnaires, disguised in civilian rebel garb, were reported to be behind major operations directed against key government buildings including Gaddafi's Bab al-Aziziya compound in central Tripoli.

Reports confirm that British SAS were on the ground in Eastern Libya prior to the onset of the air campaign. Special Forces were in close coordination with NATO air operations.

> Highly-trained units, known as 'Smash' teams for their prowess and destructive ability, have carried out secret reconnaissance missions to provide up-to-date information on the Libyan armed forces.[1]

NATO special forces and the CIA sponsored Islamic brigades under the command of "former" jihadists constituted the backbone of combat capabilities on the ground, supported by NATO's air campaign.

The remainder of the rebel forces included untrained trigger happy gunmen (including teenagers) who served the function of creating an atmosphere of panic and intimidation.

What we are dealing with is a carefully planned military-intelligence operation to invade and occupy a sovereign country.

Intensive Bombing Raids over Tripoli

By late August 2011, barely a week before the "Liberation" of Tripoli, NATO acknowledged the conduct of more than twenty thousand sorties since the outset of the war in March 2011, and more than seven thousand seven hundred strike sorties. Multiply the number of strike sorties (seven thousand seven hundred sixty-eight since March 31, 2011) by the average number of missiles or bombs launched by each of the planes and you get a rough idea of the size and magnitude of this "humanitarian" military operation. A French Dassault Mirage 2000, for instance, can transport eighteen missiles under its wings. America's B-2 Stealth bombers are equipped with bunker buster bombs

Pursuant to NATO's humanitarian mandate, we were informed by the media that these tens of thousands of strikes had not resulted in civilian casualties (with the exception of occasional "collateral damage"). Not surprisingly, already in mid-April 2011, three weeks into the bombing campaign, the Atlantic Alliance announced that "NATO planes flying combat missions over Libya *are starting to run out of bombs*".

The Conquest of Libya's Oil Reserves

The endgame of the U.S.-NATO humanitarian operation –using the Libya Islamic Fighting Group (LIFG) terrorists as their foot-soldiers– was the acquisition of Libya's extensive oil reserves.

"Operation Libya" should be viewed as part of a broader military agenda in the Middle East and Central Asia which consists in gaining control and corporate ownership over more than sixty percent of the world's reserves of oil and natural gas, including oil and gas pipeline routes.

> Muslim countries including Saudi Arabia, Iraq, Iran, Kuwait, the United Arab Emirates, Qatar, Yemen, Libya, Egypt, Nigeria, Algeria, Kazakhstan, Azerbaijan, Malaysia, Indonesia, Brunei, possess between 66.2 and 75.9 percent of total oil reserves, depending on the source and methodology of the estimate.[2]

With forty-six and a half billion barrels of proven reserves, (ten times those of Egypt), Libya is the largest oil economy in the African continent followed by Nigeria and Algeria (Oil and Gas Journal). In contrast, U.S. proven oil reserves are of the order of 20.6 billion barrels (December 2008) according to the Energy Information Administration.[3]

Estimates placed Libya's oil reserves at 60 billion barrels. Its gas reserves at 1,500 billion m3. Its production was between 1.3 and 1.7 million barrels a day, well below its productive capacity. Its longer term objective was three million barrels a day and a gas production of 2,600 million cubic feet a day, according to figures of the Libya's National Oil Corporation (NOC).

The (alternative) BP Statistical Energy Survey (2008) placed Libya's proven oil reserves at 41.464 billion barrels at the end of 2007 which represents 3.34 % of the world's proven reserves.[4]

Oil is the "Trophy" of U.S.-NATO led Wars

The NATO invasion of Libya under a humanitarian mandate has broadly served the same corporate interests as the 2003 invasion and occupation of Iraq. The underlying objective was to take possession of Libya's oil reserves, destabilize the National Oil Corporation (NOC) and eventually privatize the country's oil industry, namely transfer the control and ownership of Libya's oil wealth into foreign hands.

The National Oil Corporation (NOC) was ranked twenty-fifth among the world's Top 100 Oil Companies.[5]

The 2011 invasion of Libya under a NATO humanitarian mandate was part of the broader "Battle for Oil". Close to eighty percent of Libya's oil reserves are located in the Sirte Gulf basin of Eastern Libya.

Libya is a Prize Economy. "War is good for business". Wall Street, the Anglo-American oil giants, the U.S.-EU weapons producers are the unspoken beneficiaries of the U.S.-NATO led military campaign directed against Libya.

Libyan oil is a bonanza for the Anglo-American oil giants. While the market value of crude oil is well in excess of one hundred dollars a barrel, the cost of Libyan oil is extremely low, as low as one dollar a barrel (according to one estimate). As one oil market expert commented somewhat cryptically:

> At $110 on the world market, the simple math gives Libya a $109 profit margin.[6]

Foreign Oil Interests in Libya

Foreign oil companies operating prior to the 2011 war in Libya included France's Total, Italy's ENI, The China National Petroleum Corp (CNPC), British Petroleum, the Spanish Oil consortium REPSOL, ExxonMobil, Chevron, Occidental Petroleum,

Hess, Conoco Phillips. Of significance, prior to the U.S.-NATO intervention, China played a central role in the Libyan oil industry. The China National Petroleum Corp (CNPC) had a workforce of some four hundred employees. The total Chinese workforce in Libya was of the order of thirty thousand.

Eleven percent (11%) of Libyan oil exports were channelled to China. While there are no figures on the size and importance of CNPC's production and exploration activities, there are indications that they were sizeable.

More generally, China's presence in North Africa was considered by Washington to constitute an intrusion. From a geopolitical standpoint, China was an encroachment. The military campaign directed against Libya was intent upon excluding China from North Africa.

Also of importance was the role of Italy. In 2011, ENI, the Italian oil consortium, was putting out 244,000 barrels of gas and oil, which represents almost 25 percent of Libya's total exports.[7]

Among U.S. companies in Libya, Chevron and Occidental Petroleum (Oxy) decided in late 2010 not to renew their oil and gas exploration licenses in Libya.[8] In contrast, in November 2010, Germany's oil company, R.W. DIA E signed a far-reaching agreement with Libya's National Oil Corporation (NOC) involving exploration and production sharing.[9]

The financial stakes as well as "the spoils of war" are extremely high. The military operation was also intent upon dismantling Libya's financial institutions as well as confiscating billions of dollars of Libyan financial assets deposited in Western banks.

Libya: Strategic Saharan Gateway to Central Africa

Libya has borders with several countries which are within France's sphere of influence, including Algeria, Tunisia, Niger and Chad.

Chad is potentially an oil rich economy. ExxonMobil and Chevron have interests in Southern Chad including a pipeline project. Southern Chad is a gateway into the Darfur region of Sudan, which is also strategic in view of its oil wealth.

China has oil interests in both Chad and Sudan. The China National Petroleum Corp (CNPC) signed a far-reaching agreement with the Chad government in 2007.

Niger is strategic to the United States in view of its extensive reserves of uranium. At present, France dominates the uranium industry in Niger through the French nuclear conglomerate Areva, formerly known as Cogema. China also has a stake in Niger's uranium industry.

More generally, the Southern border of Libya is strategic for the United States in its quest to extend its sphere of influence into Francophone Africa, a vast territory extending from North Africa to Central and Western Africa. Historically this region was part of France and Belgium's colonial empires, the borders of which were established at the Berlin Conference of 1884.

The U.S. played a passive role at the 1884 Berlin Conference. This new twenty-first century redivision of the African continent, predicated on the control over oil, natural gas and strategic minerals (cobalt, chromium, manganese, platinum and uranium) largely supports dominant Anglo-American corporate interests.

U.S. interference in North Africa redefines the geopolitics of an entire region. It undermines China and overshadows the influence of the European Union in Africa.

Redrawing the Map of Africa

Libya has the second largest oil reserves in Africa. The objective of U.S.-NATO interference is strategic: it consists in outright theft, in stealing the nation's oil wealth under the disguise of a humanitarian intervention.

This military operation was intent upon establishing U.S. hegemony in North Africa, a region historically dominated by France and to lesser extent by Italy and Spain.

With regard to Tunisia, Morocco and Algeria, Washington's design is to weaken the political links of these countries to France and push for the installation of new political regimes which have a close rapport with the U.S.. This weakening of France is part of a U.S. imperial design. It is a historical process which goes back to the wars in Indochina.

U.S.-NATO intervention leading to the eventual formation of a U.S. puppet regime in Libya is also intent upon excluding China from the region and edging out China's National Petroleum Corp

(CNPC). The Anglo-American oil giants including British Petroleum which signed an exploration contract in 2007 with the Gaddafi government are among the potential "beneficiaries" of the U.S.-NATO military operation.

The Endgame is to Exclude France

More generally, what is at stake is the redrawing of the map of Africa, a process of neocolonial redivision, the scrapping of the demarcations of the 1884 Berlin Conference, the conquest of Africa by the United States in alliance with Britain, in a U.S.-NATO led operation.

While France intervenes militarily in Africa in coordination and on behalf of Washington, the end-game is to eventually exclude France from both the Maghreb and sub-Saharan Africa. While the U.S. is prepared in the short-run to share the spoils of war with France, Washington's ultimate objective is to "redraw the map of the African continent" and eventually to transform francophone Africa into an American sphere of influence. The latter would extend across the continent from Mauritania on the Atlantic to the Sudan, Ethiopia and Somalia.

A similar process of *excluding France from francophone Africa* has been ongoing since the 1990s in Rwanda, Burundi and the Republic of the Congo.

In turn, French as an official language in francophone Africa is being encroached upon. Today in Rwanda, English is an official language, alongside Kinyarwanda and French. Starting with the RPF government in 1994, secondary education was offered in either French or English. Since 2009, it is offered solely in English. The University since 1994, no longer operates in French. (The president of Rwanda Paul Kagame does not read or speak French.) In 2009, Rwanda joined the Commonwealth.

What is at stake is a vast territory which during the colonial period included French West Africa and French Equatorial Africa

Mali during the French period was referred to as *Le Soudan français* (the French Sudan).

Ironically, this process of weakening and *eventually excluding France from francophone Africa* has been carried out with the tacit endorsement of both (former) president Nicolas Sarkozy and president François Hollande, both of whom are serving U.S. geopolitical interests to the detriment of the French Republic.

The militarization of the African continent is part of the mandate of U.S. Africa Command (AFRICOM).

The longer term goal is to exert geopolitical as well as military control over a vast area, which historically has been within France's sphere of influence. This area is an rich in oil, natural gas, gold, uranium and strategic minerals.[10]

This new redivision of Africa not only weakens the role of the former colonial powers (including France and Italy) in North Africa. it is also part of a broader process of displacing and weakening France (and Belgium) over a large part of the African continent.

U.S. puppet regimes have been installed in several African countries which historically were in the sphere of influence of France (and Belgium), including The Republic of the Congo and Rwanda. Several countries in West Africa are slated to become U.S. proxy states.

The European Union is heavily dependent on the flow of Libyan oil. Eighty-five percent of its oil is sold to European countries. Thirty percent of Italy's oil and ten percent of its gas are imported from Libya. Libyan gas is fed through the Greenstream pipeline in the Mediterranean.

The heads of state and heads of government of NATO countries are the architects of war and destruction in Libya, Syria, Iraq and Afghanistan. In an utterly twisted logic, they are heralded as the voices of reason, as the representatives of the "international community". Realities are turned upside down. A humanitarian intervention is launched by war criminals in high office, who are the unchallenged guardians of the Just War theory.

Libya was targeted because it is one among several remaining countries outside America's sphere of influence, which failed to conform to U.S. demands. Libya is a country which was selected as part of a military "road map" which consists of "multiple simultaneous theater wars".

Notes

1. SAS 'Smash' squads on the ground in Libya to mark targets for coalition jets, *Daily Mirror*, March 21, 2011.
2. See Michel Chossudovsky, The "Demonization" of Muslims and the Battle for Oil, Global Research, January 4, 2007.
3. U.S. Crude Oil, Natural Gas, and Natural Gas Liquids Reserves.
4. Mbendi Oil and Gas in Libya – Overview, 2011.
5. The Energy Intelligence ranks Libya's NOC 25 among the world's Top 100 companies. Libyaonline.com.
6. Libya Oil, Libya Oil One Country's $109 Profit on $110 Oil, EnergyandCapital.com, March 12, 2008.
7. Sky News: Foreign oil firms halt Libyan operations, February 23, 2011.
8. Why are Chevron and Oxy leaving Libya? Voice of Russia, October 6, 2010.
9. AfricaNews – Libya: German oil firm signs prospecting deal – The AfricaNews website.
10. R. Teichman, The War on Mali. What you Should Know: An Eldorado of Uranium, Gold, Petroleum, Strategic Minerals, Global Research, January 15, 2013.

An earlier version of this chapter was published in March 2011 prior to the war on Libya. Minor corrections and additions have been made.

America's War on Iraq and Syria: Terrorism with a "Human Face" The History of America's Death Squads

Death Squads in Iraq and Syria. The Historical Roots of U.S.-NATO's Covert War on Syria

T*he recruitment of death squads is part of a well-established U.S. military-intelligence agenda. There is a long and grue-some U.S. history of covert funding and support of terror brigades and targeted assassinations going back to the Vietnam war.*

As government forces continue to confront the self-proclaimed "Free Syrian Army" (FSA) and its affiliated rebel forces, the his-torical roots of the West's covert war on Syria –which has resulted in countless atrocities– must be fully revealed.

From the outset in March 2011, the U.S. and its allies have sup- ported the formation of death squads and the incursion of terrorist brigades in a carefully planned undertaking.

The recruitment and training of terror brigades in both Iraq and Syria was modeled on the "Salvador Option", a "terrorist model" of mass killings by U.S. sponsored death squads in Central America. It was first applied in El Salvador, in the heyday of resistance against the military dictatorship, resulting in an estimated seventy-five thou-sand deaths.

The formation of death squads in Syria builds upon the history and experience of U.S. sponsored terror brigades in Iraq, under the Pentagon's "counter-insurgency" program.

The Establishment of Death Squads in Iraq

U.S. sponsored death squads were recruited in Iraq starting in 2004-2005 in an initiative launched under the helm of the U.S. Ambassador John Negroponte, who was dispatched to Baghdad by the U.S. State Department in June 2004.

Negroponte was the "man for the job". As U.S. Ambassador to Honduras from 1981 to 1985. Negroponte played a key role in supporting and supervising the Nicaraguan Contras based in Honduras as well as overseeing the activities of the Honduran military death squads.

"Under the rule of General Gustavo Alvarez Martinez, Honduras's military government was both a close ally of the Reagan administration and was (disappearing) dozens of political opponents in classic death squad fashion."

In January 2005, the Pentagon, confirmed that it was considering:

> *... forming hit squads of Kurdish and Shia fighters* to target leaders of the Iraqi insurgency [Resistance] in a strategic shift *borrowed from the American struggle against left-wing guerrillas in Central America 20 years ago."*
> *Under the so-called "El Salvador option", Iraqi and American forces would be sent to kill or kidnap insurgency leaders, even in Syria, where some are thought to shelter. ...*
> Hit squads would be controversial and would probably be kept secret.
> The experience of the so-called "death squads" in Central America remains raw for many even now and helped to sully the image of the United States in the region.
> Then, the Reagan Administration funded and trained teams of nationalist forces to neutralize Salvadorean rebel leaders and sympathizers. ...
> John Negroponte, the U.S. Ambassador in Baghdad, had a front-row seat at the time as Ambassador to Honduras from 1981-85.
> Death squads were a brutal feature of Latin American politics of the time. ...
> In the early 1980s President Reagan's Administration funded and helped to train Nicaraguan contras based in Honduras with the aim of ousting Nicaragua's Sandinista regime. *The Contras were equipped using money from illegal American arms sales to Iran, a scandal that could have toppled Mr Reagan.*

*The thrust of the Pentagon proposal in Iraq, ... is to follow
that model. ... It is unclear whether the main aim of the missions would be to assassinate the rebels or kidnap them* and
take them away for interrogation. *Any mission in Syria
would probably be undertaken by U.S. Special Forces.*
Nor is it clear who would take responsibility for such a program –the Pentagon or the Central Intelligence Agency.
Such covert operations have traditionally been run by the
CIA at arm's length from the administration in power, giving U.S. officials the ability to deny knowledge of it.[1]

While the stated objective of the "Iraq Salvador Option" was to
"take out the insurgency", in practice the U.S. sponsored terror
brigades were involved in routine killings of civilians with a view to
fomenting sectarian violence. In turn, the CIA and MI6 were overseeing "Al Qaeda in Iraq" units involved in targeted assassinations directed against the Shiite population. Of significance, the death squads
were integrated and advised by undercover U.S. Special Forces.

Robert Stephen Ford –subsequently appointed U.S. Ambassador
to Syria– was part of Negroponte's team in Baghdad in 2004-2005.
In January 2004, he was dispatched as U.S. representative to the Shiite city of Najaf which was the stronghold of the Mahdi army, with
which he made preliminary contacts.

In January 2005, Robert S. Ford's was appointed Minister Coun-
selor for Political Affairs at the U.S. Embassy under the helm of Ambassador John Negroponte. He was not only part of the inner team,
he was Negroponte's partner in setting up the Salvador Option for
Iraq. Some of the groundwork had been established in Najaf prior to
Ford's transfer to Baghdad.

John Negroponte and Robert Stephen Ford were put in charge of
recruiting the Iraqi death squads. While Negroponte coordinated the
operation from his office at the U.S. Embassy, Robert S. Ford, who
was fluent in both Arabic and Turkish, was entrusted with the task
of establishing strategic contacts with Shiite and Kurdish militia
groups outside the "Green Zone".

Two other embassy officials, namely *Henry Ensher* (Ford's
Deputy) and a younger official in the political section, *Jeffrey Beals*,
played an important role in the team "talking to a range of Iraqis, in-

cluding extremists".[2] Another key individual in Negroponte's team was *James Franklin Jeffrey*, America's ambassador to Albania (2002-2004). In 2010, Jeffrey was appointed U.S. Ambassador to Iraq (2010-2012).

Negroponte also brought into the team one of his former collaborators *Colonel James Steele* (ret) from his Honduras heyday:

Under the "Salvador Option," "Negroponte had assistance from his colleague from his days in Central America during the 1980's, retired *Col James Steele.*"

> *Steele, whose title in Baghdad was Counselor for Iraqi Security Forces supervised the selection and training of members of the Badr Organization and Mehdi Army*, the two largest Shi'ite militias in Iraq, in order to target the leadership and support networks of a primarily Sunni resistance. Planned or not, these death squads promptly spiraled out of control to become the leading cause of death in Iraq.
>
> Intentional or not, the scores of tortured, mutilated bodies which turn up on the streets of Baghdad each day are *generated by the death squads whose impetus was John Negroponte. And it is this U.S.-backed sectarian violence which largely led to the hell-disaster that Iraq is today.*[3]

Colonel Steele was responsible, according to Rep. Dennis Kucinich for implementing "a plan in El Salvador under which tens of thousands Salvadorans (disappeared) or were murdered, including Archbishop Oscar Romero and four American nuns."[4]

Upon his appointment to Baghdad, Colonel Steele was assigned to a counter-insurgency unit known as the "Special Police Commando" under the Iraqi Interior Ministry"[5]

Reports confirm that "the U.S. military turned over many prisoners to the *Wolf Brigade*, the feared 2nd battalion of the interior ministry's special commandos" which so happened to be under the supervision of Colonel Steele:

> U.S. soldiers, U.S. advisers, *were standing aside and doing nothing, while members of the Wolf Brigade beat and tortured prisoners.* The interior ministry commandos took over the public library in Samarra, and turned it into a detention

centre, he said. An interview conducted by Maass [of the New York Times] in 2005 at the improvised prison, accompanied by the Wolf Brigade's U.S. military adviser, Colonel James Steele, had been interrupted by the terrified . screams of a prisoner outside, he said. Steele was reportedly previously employed as an adviser to help crush an insurgency in El Salvador.[6]

Another notorious figure –who played a role in Iraq's counter-insurgency program– was Former New York Police Commissioner *Bernie Kerik* who in 2007 was indicted in federal court on sixteen felony charges.

Kerik had been appointed by the Bush administration at the outset of the occupation in 2003 to assist in the organization and training of the Iraqi Police force. During his short stint in 2003, Bernie Kerik –who took on the position of interim Minister of the Interior– worked towards organizing terror units within the Iraqi Police force:

> Dispatched to Iraq to whip Iraqi security forces into shape, Kerik dubbed himself the "interim interior minister of Iraq." *British police advisors called him the "Baghdad terminator."*[7]

Under Negroponte's helm at the U.S. Embassy in Baghdad, a wave of covert civilian killings and targeted assassinations had been unleashed. Engineers, medical doctors, scientists and intellectuals were also targeted.

Author and geopolitical analyst Max Fuller has documented in detail the atrocities committed under the U.S. sponsored counter-insurgency program:

> The appearance of death squads was first highlighted in May this year [2005], ...dozens of bodies were found casually disposed ... in vacant areas around Baghdad. All of the victims had been handcuffed, blindfolded and shot in the head and many of them also showed signs of having been brutally tortured. ...
> The evidence was sufficiently compelling for the Association of Muslim Scholars (AMS), a leading Sunni organization, to issue public statements in which they accused the security forces attached to the Ministry of the Interior as

well as the Badr Brigade, the former armed wing of the Supreme Council for Islamic Revolution in Iraq (SCIRI), of being behind the killings. They also accused the Ministry of the Interior of conducting state terrorism.[8]

The Police Commandos as well as the Wolf Brigade were overseen by the U.S. counter-insurgency program in the Iraqi Ministry of the Interior:

> *The Police Commandos were formed under the experienced tutelage and oversight of veteran U.S. counter-insurgency fighters*, and from the outset conducted joint-force operations with *elite and highly secretive U.S. special-forces units.*[9]

James Steele was a k*ey figure in the development of the "Special Police Commandos"*:

> Another U.S. contributor was the same *Steven Casteel* who as the most senior U.S. advisor within the Interior Ministry brushed off serious and well-substantiated accusations of appalling human right violations as 'rumor and innuendo'. Like Steele, Casteel gained considerable experience in Latin America, in his case participating in the hunt for the cocaine baron Pablo Escobar in Colombia's Drugs Wars of the 1990s. …
>
> Casteel's background is significant because this kind of intelligence-gathering support role and the production of death lists are characteristic of U.S. involvement in counterinsurgency programs and constitute the underlying thread in what can appear to be random, disjointed killing sprees.
>
> Such *centrally planned genocides* are entirely consistent with what is taking place in Iraq today [2005] …It is also consistent with what little we know about the Special Police Commandos, which was tailored to provide the Interior Ministry with a special-forces strike capability (U.S. Department of Defense). In keeping with such a role, the Police Commando headquarters has become the hub of a nationwide command, control, communications, computer and intelligence operations centre, courtesy of the U.S.[10]

This initial groundwork established under Negroponte in 2005 was implemented under his successor Ambassador Zalmay Khalilzad. Robert Stephen Ford ensured the continuity of the project prior to his appointment as U.S. Ambassador to Algeria in 2006, as well as upon his return to Baghdad as Deputy Chief of Mission in 2008.

Operation "Syrian Contras": Learning from the Iraqi Experience

The gruesome Iraqi version of the "Salvador Option" under the helm of Ambassador John Negroponte had served as a "role model" for setting up the "Free Syrian Army" Contras in Syria as well as the Al Nusrah and The Islamic State of Iraq and the Levant (ISIL). Robert Stephen Ford was, no doubt, involved in the preparation of the Syrian Contras project, following his reassignment to Baghdad as Deputy Head of Mission in 2008.

The Islamic State (ISIS) "Made in America"

The U.S. is taking advantage of the incontestable threat posed by the brutal "IS" combatants in order to polish their damaged image in the Middle East and simultaneously try to underline that their further military presence in the region is indispensable.

At the same time, the virtual inventor of the "IS" is none other than former U.S. Secretary of State Condoleezza Rice. In 2006, during the peak of the U.S.–Iran conflict, she prompted all Sunni states to set up a "Sunni belt" in response to the alleged "Shia belt" that Iran had supposedly created against Arab Sunnis. ... Then the Secretary-General of the Saudi National Security Council, the infamous Prince Bandar bin Sultan, set to work. The results were the birth of brutal groups such as the Al-Nusra Front and "ISIS", which sprang up like mushrooms to fight the Assad regime in Syria. In the final analysis, the outcome of the 2006 Condoleezza Rice plan was also the creation of the barbaric "IS" group, which is unprecedented in the entire history of Islam.

Prof. Mohssen Massarrat, The Fiction of "Fighting the Islamic State", An Entity Created and Financed by the U.S. and Saudi Arabia, Global Research, September 2, 2014.

The objective in Syria was to create factional divisions between Sunni, Alawite, Shiite, Kurds, Druze and Christians. While the Syrian context is entirely different to that of Iraq, there are striking similarities with regard to the procedures whereby the killings and atrocities were conducted.

A report published by *Der Spiegel* pertaining to atrocities committed in the Syrian city of Homs confirms an organized sectarian process of mass-murder and extra-judicial killings comparable to that conducted by the U.S. sponsored death squads in Iraq.

People in Homs were routinely categorized as "prisoners" (Shia, Alawite) and "traitors". The "traitors" are Sunni civilians within the rebel occupied urban area, who expressed their disagreement or opposition to the rule of terror of the Free Syrian Army (FSA):

> *"Since last summer [2011], we have executed slightly fewer than 150 men, which represents about 20 percent of our prisoners,"* says Abu Rami. ... But the executioners of Homs have been busier with traitors within their own ranks than with prisoners of war. "If we catch a Sunni spying, or if a citizen betrays the revolution, *we make it quick,"* says the fighter. *According to Abu Rami, Hussein's burial brigade has put between 200 and 250 traitors to death since the beginning of the uprising.*[11]

The project required an initial program of recruitment and training of mercenaries. Death squads including Lebanese and Jordanian Salafist units entered Syria's southern border with Jordan in mid-March 2011. Much of the groundwork was already in place prior to Robert Stephen Ford's arrival in Damascus in January 2011.

Ford's appointment as Ambassador to Syria was announced in early 2010. Diplomatic relations had been cut in 2005 following the Rafick Hariri assassination, which Washington blamed on Syria. Ford arrived in Damascus barely two months before the onset of the insurgency.

The Free Syrian Army (FSA)

Washington and its allies replicated in Syria the essential features of the "Iraq Salvador Option", leading to the creation of the

Free Syrian Army (FSA) and its various terrorist factions including the Al Qaeda affiliated Al Nusra and ISIL brigades.

While the creation of the Free Syrian Army (FSA) was announced in June 2011, the recruitment and training of foreign mercenaries was initiated at a much earlier period.

In many regards, the Free Syrian Army was a smokescreen. It was upheld by the Western media as a bona fide military entity established as a result of mass defections from government forces. The number of defectors, however, was neither significant nor sufficient to establish a coherent military structure with command and control functions.

The FSA was not a professional military entity, Rather it was a loose network of separate terrorist brigades, which in turn are made up of numerous paramilitary cells operating in different parts of the country

Each of these terrorist organizations operates independently. The FSA did not effectively exercise command and control functions including liaison with these diverse paramilitary entities. The latter are controlled by U.S.-NATO sponsored special forces and intelligence operatives which are embedded within the ranks of selected terrorist formations.

These (highly trained) Special Forces on the ground (many of whom are employees of private security companies) were routinely in contact with U.S.-NATO and allied military/intelligence command units (including Turkey). These embedded Special Forces were, no doubt, also involved in the carefully planned bomb attacks directed against government buildings, military compounds, etc.

The death squads are mercenaries trained and recruited by the U.S., NATO, America's Persian Gulf GCC allies as well as Turkey. The death squads are overseen by allied special forces (including British SAS and French Parachutistes), and private security companies on contract to NATO and the Pentagon. In this regard, reports confirm the arrest by the Syrian government of some 200-300 private security company employees who had integrated rebel ranks.

The Jabhat Al Nusra Front

The Al Nusra Front –which is said to be affiliated to Al Qaeda– together with the *Islamic State of Iraq and the Levant (ISIL)* are described as the most effective "opposition" rebel fighting group, responsible for several of the high profile bomb attacks. Portrayed as an enemy of America (on the State Department list of terrorist organizations), Al Nusra and ISIL operations, nonetheless, bear the fingerprints of U.S. paramilitary training, terror tactics and weapons systems. The atrocities committed against civilians by Al Nusra (funded covertly by U.S.-NATO) are similar to those undertaken by the U.S. sponsored death squads in Iraq.

In the words of Al Nusra leader Abu Adnan in Aleppo:

> Jabhat al-Nusra does count Syrian veterans of the Iraq war among its numbers, men who bring expertise –especially the manufacture of improvised explosive devices (IEDs)– to the front in Syria.

As in Iraq, factional violence and ethnic cleansing were actively promoted. In Syria, the Alawite, Shiite and Christian communities were the target of the U.S.-NATO sponsored death squads. The Alawite and the Christian community are the main targets of the assassination program. Confirmed by the Vatican News Service:

> Christians in Aleppo are victims of death and destruction due to the fighting which for months, has been affecting the city. The Christian neighborhoods, in recent times, have been hit by rebel forces fighting against the regular army and this has caused an exodus of civilians.
> Some groups in the rugged opposition, where there are also jihadist groups, "fire on Christian houses and buildings, to force occupants to escape and then take possession [ethnic cleansing][12]

> The Sunni Salafist militants – says the Bishop – continue to commit crimes against civilians, or to recruit fighters with force. The fanatical Sunni extremists are fighting a holy war proudly, especially against the Alawites. When terrorists seek to control the religious identity of a suspect, they ask him to cite the genealogies dating back to Moses. And they ask to recite a prayer that the Alawites removed. The Alawites have no chance to get out alive.[13]

Reports also confirm the influx of Salafist and Al Qaeda affiliated death squads as well as brigades under the auspices of the Muslim Brotherhood into Syria from the inception of the insurgency in March 2011.

Moreover, reminiscent of the enlistment of the Mujahideen to wage the CIA's jihad (holy war) in the heyday of the Soviet-Afghan war, NATO and the Turkish High command, according to Israeli intelligence sources, had initiated:

> *A campaign to enlist thousands of Muslim volunteers in Middle East countries and the Muslim world to fight alongside the Syrian rebels. The Turkish army would house these volunteers, train them and secure their passage into Syria.*[14]

The Role of Saudi Arabia and Qatar

Amply documented, U.S.-NATO support to Al Nusrah and the Islamic State (IS) in Syria is channeled covertly through America's staunchest allies: Qatar and Saudi Arabia. Acknowledged by the Western media, both Riyadh and Doha acting in liaison and on behalf of Washington have played a central role in the financing the various jihadist formations including al Nusrah and the Islamic State (IS) as well as the recruitment, training and religious indoctrination of terrorist mercenary forces deployed in Syria.

According to London's Daily Express *"They [the Islamic State terrorists] had money and arms supplied by Qatar and Saudi Arabia."*

> The most important source of ISIS financing to date has been support coming out of the Gulf states, primarily Saudi Arabia but also Qatar, Kuwait and the United Arab Emirates,[15]

This money was channeled to ISIS terrorists fighting against government forces in Syria:

> *Through allies such as Saudi Arabia and Qatar, the West [has] supported militant rebel groups* which have since mutated into ISIS and other al-Qaeda connected militias.[16]

According to Robert Fisk, the IS caliphate project "has been bankrolled by Saudi Arabia":

[M]eet *Saudi Arabia's latest monstrous contribution to world history: the Islamist Sunni caliphate of Iraq and the Levant,* conquerors of Mosul and Tikrit – and Raqqa in Syria – and possibly Baghdad, and the ultimate humiliators of Bush and Obama.

From Aleppo in northern Syria almost to the Iraqi-Iranian border, the jihadists of Isis and sundry other groupuscules paid by the Saudi Wahhabis –and by Kuwaiti oligarchs– now rule thousands of square miles.[17]

In 2013, as part of its recruitment of terrorists, Saudi Arabia took the initiative of releasing prisoners on death row in Saudi jails.

A secret memo revealed that the prisoners were being "recruited" to join jihadist militia (including Al Nusra and ISIS) to fight against government forces in Syria.

The prisoners had reportedly been offered a deal: stay and be executed or fight against Assad in Syria. As part of the deal the prisoners were offered a "pardon and a monthly stipend for their families, who were allowed to stay in the Sunni Arab kingdom".

Saudi officials apparently gave them a choice: decapitation or jihad? In total, inmates from Yemen, Palestine, Saudi Arabia, Sudan, Syria, Jordan, Somalia, Afghanistan, Egypt, Pakistan, Iraq, and Kuwait chose to go and fight in Syria.[18]

Private Security Companies and the Recruitment of Mercenaries

According to reports, private security companies operating out of the Gulf States have been involved in the recruitment and training of mercenaries. Reports point to the creation of training camps in Qatar and the United Arab Emirates (UAE).

In Zayed Military City (UAE), "a secret army is in the making" operated by Xe Services, formerly Blackwater. The UAE deal to establish a military camp for the training of mercenaries was signed in July 2010, nine months before the onslaught of the wars in Libya and Syria.

Confirmed by CNN, security companies on contract to NATO and the Pentagon were involved in training "opposition" death squads in the use of chemical weapons:

"The United States and some European allies *are using defense contractors to train Syrian rebels on how to secure chemical weapons stockpiles in Syria*", a senior U.S. official and several senior diplomats told CNN Sunday.[19]

The names of the companies involved were not revealed.

Behind Closed Doors at the U.S. State Department

Robert Stephen Ford was part of a small team at the U.S. State Department team which oversaw the recruitment and training of terrorist brigades, together with *Derek Chollet* and *Frederic C. Hof,* a former business partner of Richard Armitage, who served as Washington's "special coordinator on Syria". Derek Chollet was appointed to the position of Assistant Secretary of Defense for International Security Affairs (ISA).

This team operated under the helm of (former) Assistant Secretary of State for Near Eastern Affairs Jeffrey Feltman.

Feltman's team was in close liaison with the process of recruitment and training of mercenaries out of Turkey, Qatar, Saudi Arabia and Libya courtesy of the post-Gaddafi regime, which dispatched six hundred Libya Islamic Fighting Group (LIFG) troops to Syria, via Turkey in the months following the September 2011 collapse of the Gaddafi government.[20]

> Assistant Secretary of State Feltman was in contact with Saudi Foreign Minister Prince *Saud al-Faisal*, and Qatari Foreign Minister *Sheikh Hamad bin Jassim*. He was also in charge of a Doha-based office for "special security coordination" pertaining to Syria, which included representatives from Western and GCC intelligence agencies as well as a representative from Libya. *Prince Bandar bin Sultan.* a prominent and controversial member of Saudi intelligence was part of this group.[21]

In June 2012, Jeffrey Feltman was appointed UN Under-Secretary-General for Political Affairs, a strategic position which, in practice, consists in setting the UN agenda (on behalf of Washington) on issues pertaining to "Conflict Resolution" in various "political hot spots" around the world (including Somalia, Lebanon, Libya, Syria,

Yemen and Mali). In a bitter irony, the countries for UN "Ronflict Resolution" are those which are the target of U.S. covert operations.

In liaison with the U.S. State Department, NATO and his GCC handlers in Doha and Riyadh, Feltman was Washington's man behind UN special envoy Lakhdar Brahmi's "Peace Proposal".

Meanwhile, while paying lip service to the UN Peace initiative, the U.S. and NATO had speeded up the process of recruitment and training of mercenaries in response to the heavy casualties incurred by "opposition" rebel forces.

The U.S. proposed "end game" in Syria is not regime change, but the destruction of Syria as a Nation State.

The deployment of "opposition" death squads with a mandate to kill civilians is part of this criminal undertaking.

"Terrorism with a Human Face" is upheld by the United Nations Human Rights Council, which constitutes a mouthpiece for NATO "Humanitarian Interventions" under the doctrine of "Responsibility to Protect" (R2P).

The atrocities committed by the U.S.-NATO death squads are casually blamed on the government of Bashar Al Assad. According to UN Human Rights Council High Commissioner Navi Pillay:

> This massive loss of life could have been avoided if the Syrian Government had chosen to take a different path than one of ruthless suppression of what were initially peaceful and legitimate protests by unarmed civilians,[22]

Washington's "unspoken objective" consists in breaking up Syria as a sovereign nation –along ethnic and religious lines– into several separate and "independent" political entities.

Notes

1. El Salvador-style 'death squads' to be deployed by U.S. against Iraq militants – Times Online, January 10, 2005, emphasis added.
2. See *The New Yorker*, March 26, 2007.
3. Dahr Jamail, Managing Escalation: Negroponte and Bush's New Iraq Team, Antiwar.com, January 7, 2007.

4. See Mike Whitney, Inpunity, Information Clearing House, April 9, 2006. This article contains Rep. Dennis Kucinich's letter addressed to Defense Secretary Donald Rumsfeld dated April 5, 2006.

5. See ACN, Havana, June 14, 2006.

6. *Ibid.*, emphasis added.

7. Sidney Blumenthal, The "Terminator" of Baghdad, *Salon*, December 9, 2004, emphasis added.

8. Max Fuller, Crying Wolf: Media Disinformation and Death Squads in Occupied Iraq, Global Research, November 10, 2005
http://www.globalresearch.ca/crying-wolf-media-disinformation-and-death-squads-in-occupied-iraq/1230.

9. Reuters, National Review Online, emphasis added.

10. Max Fuller, *op cit.*

11 Ulricke Putz, The Burial Brigade of Homs: An Executioner for Syria's Rebels Tells His Story, *Der Spiegel*, March 30, 2012.

12. Agenzia Fides, Vatican News Service, October 19, 2012.

13. Agenzia Fides, Vatican News Service, June 6, 2012.

14. NATO to give rebels anti-tank weapons", DEBKAfile, 'August 14, 2011.

15. According to Dr. Günter Meyer, Director of the Center for Research into the Arabic World at University of Mainz, Germany, Who finances ISIS?, Deutsche Welle, June 19, 2014.

16. *Daily Telegraph*, June 12, 2014.

17. Robert Fisk, Iraq crisis: Sunni caliphate has been bankrolled by Saudi Arabia, *The Independent*, June 12, 2014.

18. Saudi Arabia: Death-row Inmates sent to fight Assad in Syria, Global Research, September 11, 2013.

19. Elise Labott, Sources: U.S. helping underwrite Syrian rebel training on securing chemical weapons, CNN Report, December 9, 2012.

20. Russia Today, Bomb voyage: 600 Libyans 'already fighting in Syria', November 29, 2011.

21. U.S., Saudi Arabia plan to destroy Syria: Report, Press TV, May 12, 2012.

22. Quoted in Stephen Lendman, UN Human Rights Report on Syria: Camouflage of U.S.-NATO Sponsored Massacres, Global Research, January 3, 2012).

An earlier version of this chapter was published in 2012.

CHAPTER X
War and Natural Gas
The Israeli Invasion and Gaza's
Offshore Gas Fields

I n the wake of the 2008-2009 invasion, Palestinian gas fields were de facto confiscated by Israel in derogation of international law

A year following "Operation Cast Lead", Tel Aviv announced the discovery of the Leviathan natural gas field in the Eastern Mediterranean "off the coast of Israel."

At the time it was "the most prominent field ever found in the sub-explored area of the Levantine Basin, which covers about 83,000 square kilometres of the eastern Mediterranean region."[1]

Coupled with Tamar field, in the same location, discovered in 2009, the prospects are for an energy bonanza for Israel, for Houston, Texas based Noble Energy and partners Delek Drilling, Avner Oil Exploration and Ratio Oil Exploration.[2]

The Gazan gas fields are part of the broader Levant assessment area.

What is now unfolding is the integration of these adjoining gas fields including those belonging to Palestine into the orbit of Israel. (see map below, source U.S. Geological Survey).

It should be noted that the entire Eastern Mediterranean coastline extending from Egypt's Sinai to Syria constitutes an area encompassing large gas as well as oil reserves.

The December 2008-2009 military invasion of the Gaza Strip by Israeli Forces under "Operation Cast Lead" had set the stage for the derogation of Palestinian sovereign rights over its maritime border. The July-August 2014 attack under "Operation Protective Edge" (OPE) was based on a similar logic. Both operations bear a direct relationship to the control and ownership of strategic offshore gas reserves.

Operation Protective Edge is reminiscent of the infamous 2001 Dagan Plan entitled "Operation Justified Vengeance" in which the *deaths of innocent Israeli civilians had been envisaged and foreseen by IDF military planners.*

The deaths are then used to muster the support of the Israeli public as well as provide a justification for a "legitimate" counter-terrorism operation in the eyes of the international community directed against the Palestinian occupied territories.

Contrived behind closed doors in July 2001, the Dagan Plan (named after Mossad chief Meir Dagan) was slated by its IDF and Mossad architects to be "launched immediately following the next high-casualty suicide bombing, would last about a month and is expected to result in the death of hundreds of Israelis and thousands of Palestinians."[3]

"*Operation Protective Edge*" (OPE) directed against Gaza was planned well in advance of the kidnapping and murder of the three Israeli teenagers. Prime Minister Netanyahu had called up 40,000 reservists. In the wake of the shelling and bombing raids, a major ground operation scenario was envisaged.

Moreover, similar to the logic of the Dagan Plan, the head of Israeli intelligence (Mossad) had "predicted" the kidnapping of the three teenagers. Under the title Mossad chief's chillingly prescient kidnap prophecy, Haaretz confirmed that

> Mossad chief Tamir Pardo had "*outlined a scenario that was spookily* [sic] *similar to the kidnapping of three teens missing in the West Bank*[3]

Israeli civilian deaths are blamed on Hamas without evidence to justify military action against Gaza.

Gaza's Extensive Offshore Gas Reserves

This is a war of conquest. The hidden agenda is the confiscation of Gaza's offshore gas fields. The ultimate objective of "Operation Protective Edge" is to break the institutional base of the Hamas leadership and destroy Gaza's civilian infrastructure, with a view to eventually carrying out the annexation of the Gaza Strip to Israel.

Discovered in 2000, there are extensive gas reserves off the Gaza coastline.

British Gas (BG Group) and its partner, the Athens based Consolidated Contractors International Company (CCC) owned by Lebanon's Sabbagh and Koury families, were granted oil and gas exploration rights in a twenty-five year agreement signed in November 1999 with the Palestinian Authority.

The rights to the offshore gas field were respectively British Gas (sixty percent); Consolidated Contractors (CCC) (thirty percent); and the Investment Fund of the Palestinian Authority (ten percent).[5]

The PA-BG-CCC agreement included field development and the construction of a gas pipeline. The BG license covered the entire Gazan offshore marine area, which is contiguous to several Israeli offshore gas facilities. (See map below). It should be noted that sixty percent of the gas reserves along the Gaza-Israel coastline belong to Palestine.

The BG Group drilled two wells in 2000: *Gaza Marine-1 and Gaza Marine-2*. Reserves are estimated by British Gas to be of the order of 1.4 trillion cubic feet, valued at approximately four billion dollars. These are the figures made public by British Gas. The size of Palestine's gas reserves could be much larger.

Who Owns the Gas Fields

The issue of sovereignty over Gaza's gas fields is crucial. From a legal standpoint, the gas reserves belong to Palestine.

The death of Yasser Arafat, the election of the Hamas government and the ruin of the Palestinian Authority have enabled Israel to establish de facto control over Gaza's offshore gas reserves.

British Gas (BG Group) has been dealing with the Tel Aviv government. In turn, the Hamas government has been bypassed in regards to exploration and development rights over the gas fields.

The election of Prime Minister Ariel Sharon in 2001 was a major turning point. Palestine's sovereignty over the offshore gas fields was challenged in the Israeli Supreme Court. Sharon stated unequivocally that "Israel would never buy gas from Palestine" intimating that Gaza's offshore gas reserves belong to Israel.

In 2003, Ariel Sharon, vetoed an initial deal, which would allow British Gas to supply Israel with natural gas from Gaza's offshore wells.[6]

The election victory of Hamas in 2006 was conducive to the demise of the Palestinian Authority, which became confined to the West Bank, under the proxy regime of Mahmoud Abbas.

In 2006, British Gas "was close to signing a deal to pump the gas to Egypt."[7] According to reports, British Prime Minister Tony Blair intervened on behalf of Israel with a view to shunting the agreement with Egypt.

The following year, in May 2007, the Israeli Cabinet approved a proposal by Prime Minister Ehud Olmert "to buy gas from the Palestinian Authority". The proposed contract was for four billion dollars, with profits of the order of two billion dollars of which one billion was to go the Palestinians.

Tel Aviv, however, had no intention of sharing the revenues with Palestine. An Israeli team of negotiators was set up by the Israeli Cabinet to thrash out a deal with the BG Group, bypassing both the Hamas government and the Palestinian Authority:

> *Israeli defense authorities want the Palestinians to be paid*
> *in goods and services and insist that no money go to the*
> *Hamas-controlled Government.*[8]

The objective was essentially to nullify the contract signed in 1999 between the BG Group and the Palestinian Authority under Yasser Arafat.

Under the proposed 2007 agreement with BG, Palestinian gas from Gaza's offshore wells was to be channeled by an undersea pipeline to the Israeli seaport of Ashkelon, thereby transferring control over the sale of the natural gas to Israel.

The deal fell through. The negotiations were suspended: "Mossad Chief Meir Dagan opposed the transaction on security grounds, that the proceeds would fund terror".[9]

Israel's intent was to foreclose the possibility that royalties be paid to the Palestinians. In December 2007, The BG Group withdrew from the negotiations with Israel and in January 2008 they closed their office in Israel.[10]

Invasion Plan on The Drawing Board

The invasion plan of the Gaza Strip under "Operation Cast Lead" was set in motion in June 2008, according to Israeli military sources:

> Sources in the defense establishment said Defense Minister
> Ehud Barak instructed the Israel Defense Forces to prepare

for the operation over six months ago [June or before June], even as Israel was beginning to negotiate a ceasefire agreement with Hamas.[11]

That very same month, the Israeli authorities contacted British Gas, with a view to resuming crucial negotiations pertaining to the purchase of Gaza's natural gas:

> Both Ministry of Finance director general Yarom Ariav and Ministry of National Infrastructures director general Hezi Kugler agreed to inform BG of Israel's wish to renew the talks. The sources added that BG has not yet officially responded to Israel's request, but that company executives would probably come to Israel in a few weeks to hold talks with government officials.[12]

The decision to speed up negotiations with British Gas (BG Group) coincided, chronologically, with the planning of the invasion of Gaza initiated in June 2008. It would appear that Israel was anxious to reach an agreement with the BG Group prior to the invasion, which was already in an advanced planning stage.

Moreover, these negotiations with British Gas were conducted by the Ehud Olmert government with the knowledge that a military invasion of Gaza was on the drawing board.

In fact, negotiations between British Gas and Israeli officials were ongoing in October 2008, two to three months prior to the commencement of the bombings of Gaza on December 27, 2008

In November 2008, the Israeli Ministry of Finance and the Ministry of National Infrastructures instructed Israel Electric Corporation (IEC) to enter into negotiations with British Gas, on the purchase of natural gas from the BG's offshore concession in Gaza.

> Ministry of Finance director general Yarom Ariav and Ministry of National Infrastructures director general Hezi Kugler wrote to IEC CEO Amos Lasker recently, informing him of the government's decision to allow negotiations to go forward, in line with the framework proposal it approved earlier this year.

The IEC board, headed by chairman Moti Friedman, approved the principles of the framework proposal a few weeks ago. The talks with BG Group will begin once the board approves the exemption from a tender.[13]

Gaza and Energy Geopolitics

The 2008-2009 military occupation of Gaza was intent upon transferring the sovereignty of the gas fields to Israel in violation of international law. The followup on July 2014 of Protective Edge has a similar logic.

What is the intent of Israel with regard to Palestine's Natural Gas reserves? A new territorial arrangement is in the making. In the wake of the 2008, the entire Gaza coastline was militarized.

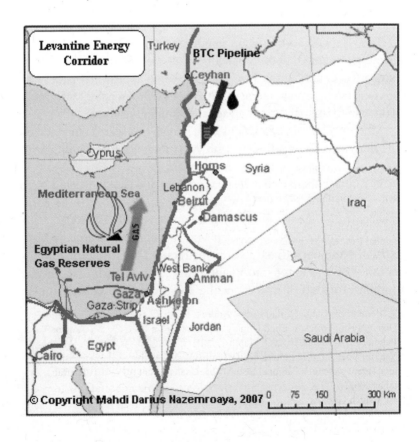

The objective of the Netanyahu government is outright confiscation of Palestinian gas fields and a de facto unilateral declaration of Israeli sovereignty over Gaza's maritime areas.

Under this scenario, the Gaza gas fields would be integrated into Israel's offshore installations, which are contiguous to those of the Gaza Strip. (See Map 1 on the opposite page).

These various offshore installations are also linked up to Israel's energy transport corridor, extending from the port of Eilat, which is an oil pipeline terminal, on the Red Sea to the seaport – pipeline terminal at Ashkelon, and northwards to Haifa, and eventually linking up through a proposed Israeli-Turkish pipeline with the Turkish port of Ceyhan.

Ceyhan is the terminal of the Baku, Tblisi Ceyhan Trans Caspian pipeline. "What is envisaged is to link the BTC pipeline to the Trans-Israel Eilat-Ashkelon pipeline, also known as Israel's Tipline."[14]

Notes

1. Leviathan Gas Field, Levantine Basin, Mediterranean Sea, Israel, offshore-technology.com.
2. Felicity Arbuthnot, Israel: Gas, Oil and Trouble in the Levant, Global Research, December 30, 2013.
3. Barak Ravid, Mossad chief's chillingly prescient kidnap prophecy, *Haaretz*, July 13, 2014, emphasis added. http://www.haaretz.com/news/diplomacy-defense/.premium-1.598751.
4. See Ellis Shuman, "Operation Justified Vengeance": a Secret Plan to Destroy the Palestinian Authority, Intelligence Ploy behind the "Suicide bombings", Global Research, February 01, 2006.
5. *Haaretz*, October 21, 2007.
6. *The Independent*, August 19, 2003.
7. *London Times*, May 23, 2007.
8. *Ibid*.
9. Member of Knesset Gilad Erdan, Address to the Knesset on "The Intention of Deputy Prime Minister Ehud Olmert to Purchase Gas from the Palestinians When Payment Will Serve Hamas," March 1, 2006, quoted in Lt. Gen. (ret.) Moshe Yaalon, Does the Prospective Purchase of British Gas from Gaza's Coastal Waters Threaten Israel's National Security? Jerusalem Center for Public Affairs, October 2007.
10. British Gas website.
11. Barak Ravid, Operation "Cast Lead": Israeli Air Force strike followed months of planning, *Haaretz*, December 27, 2008.

12. Globes online. Israel's Business Arena, June 23, 2008.
13. Globes online, November 13, 2008.
14. See Michel Chossudovsky, The War on Lebanon and the Battle for Oil, Global Research, July 23, 2006.

An earlier version of this chapter was written in early 2009.

CHAPTER XI

The U.S. has Installed a Neo-Nazi Government in Ukraine

According to the *New York Times*, *"The United States and the European Union have embraced the revolution here [Ukraine] as another* flowering of democracy, *a blow to authoritarianism and kleptocracy in the former Soviet space."*[1]

"Flowering Democracy, Revolution"? The grim realities are otherwise. What is at stake is a U.S.-EU-NATO sponsored coup d'état in blatant violation of international law.

The forbidden truth is that the West has engineered –through a carefully staged covert operation– the formation of a proxy regime integrated by neo-Nazis.

Confirmed by Assistant Secretary of State Victoria Nuland, key organizations in Ukraine including the neo-Nazi party Svoboda were generously supported by Washington: *"We have invested more than five billion dollars to help Ukraine to achieve these and other goals. ... We will continue to promote Ukraine to the future it deserves."*

The Western media has casually avoided to analyze the composition and ideological underpinnings of the government coalition. The word "Neo-Nazi" is a taboo. It has been excluded from the dictionary of mainstream media commentary. It will not appear in the pages of the *New York Times*, the *Washington Post* or *The Independent*. Journalists have been instructed not to use the term "Neo-Nazi" to designate Svoboda and the Right Sector.

Composition of the Coalition Government

We are not dealing with a transitional government in which neo-Nazi elements integrate the fringe of the coalition, which is led by the Fatherland party.

The Cabinet is not only integrated by Svoboda and Right Sector (not to mention former members of the defunct fascist UNA-UNSO), the two main neo-Nazi entities have been entrusted with key positions which grant them de facto control over the Armed Forces, Police, Justice and National Security.

While Yatsenuyk's Fatherland Party controls the majority of portfolios and Svoboda neo-Nazi leader Oleh Tyahnybok was not granted a major cabinet post (apparently at the request of Assistant Secretary of State Victoria Nuland), members of Svoboda and the Right Sector occupy key positions in the areas of Defense, Law Enforcement, Education and Economic Affairs.

Andriy Parubiy co-founder of the Neo-Nazi Social-National Party of Ukraine (subsequently renamed Svoboda) was appointed Secretary of *the National Security and National Defense Committee (RNBOU)*. (Рада національної безпеки і оборони України), a key position which overseas the Ministry of Defense, the Armed Forces, Law Enforcement, National Security and Intelligence. The RNBOU is a central decision-making body. While it is formally headed by the president, it is run by the Secretariat with a staff of one hundred eighty people including defense, intelligence and national security experts.

Parubiy was one of the main leaders behind the Orange Revolution in 2004. His organization was funded by the West. He is referred to by the Western media as the "kommandant" of the EuroMaidan movement. Andriy Parubiy together with party leader Oleh Tyahnybok is a follower of Ukrainian Nazi Stepan Bandera, who collaborated in the mass murder of Jews and Poles during World War II.

In turn, *Dmytro Yarosh*, leader of the Right Sector delegation in the parliament, was appointed Parubiy's deputy Secretary of the RNBOU.

Yarosh was the leader of the Brown Shirt neo-Nazi paramilitary during the EuroMaidan "protest" movement. He has called for disbanding the Party of the regions and the Communist Party.

The neo-Nazi party also controls the judicial process with the appointment of *Oleh Makhnitsky* of the Svoboda party to the position of prosecutor-general of Ukraine. What kind of justice will prevail with a renown Neo-Nazi in charge of the Prosecutor's Office of Ukraine?

Cabinet positions were also allocated to former members of the Neo-Nazi fringe organization Ukrainian National Assembly – Ukrainian National Self Defense (UNA-UNSO):

Tetyana Chernovol, portrayed in the Western press as a crusading investigative journalist without reference to her past involvement in the anti-Semitic UNA-UNSO, was named chair of the government's anti-corruption committee. *Dmytro Bulatov*, known for his alleged kidnapping by police, but also with UNA-UNSO connections, was appointed minister of youth and sports.

Yegor Sobolev, leader of a civic group in Independence Maidan and politically close to Yatsenyuk, *was appointed chair of the Lustration Committee, charged with purging followers of President Yanukovych from government and public life.*[2]

The Lustration Committee is to organize the Neo-Nazi witch-hunt against all opponents of the new neo-Nazi regime. The targets of the lustration campaign are people in positions of authority within the civil service, regional and municipal governments, education, research, etc. The term lustration refers to the "mass disqualification" of people associated with the former government. It also has racial overtones. It will in all likelihood be directed against Communists, Russians and members of the Jewish community.

It is important to reflect on the fact that the West, formally committed to democratic values, has not only spearheaded the demise of an elected president, it has instated a political regime integrated by neo-Nazis.

This is a proxy government which enables the U.S., NATO and the EU to interfere in Ukraine's internal affairs and dismantle its bilateral relations with the Russian Federation. It should be understood, however, that the Neo-Nazis do not ultimately call the shots. The composition of the Cabinet broadly coincides with U.S. Assistant Secretary of State Victoria Nuland's "recommendations" contained in the leaked telephone call to the U.S. ambassador to Ukraine.

Washington has chosen to spearhead neo-Nazis into positions of authority. Under a "regime of indirect rule", however, they take their orders on crucial military and foreign policy issues –including the deployment of troops directed against the Russian Federation– from the the U.S. State Department, the Pentagon and NATO.

Historical Background

America's neo-Nazi Government in Kiev is a reality. The body of evidence suggests that U.S.-NATO is involved in the crackdown on so-called "pro-Russian" activists. Western military advisers, intelligence operatives and Special Forces including mercenaries are actively involved in Kiev government's National Guard, which is controlled by the two Neo-Nazi parties.

The neo-Nazi mobs (for example, in Odessa May 2014) bear the hallmarks of U.S. sponsored terrorism (e.g Syria). The Right Sector terrorists are trained to commit atrocities against civilians. Confirmed by Germany's Bild: "Dozens of specialists from the U.S. Central Intelligence Agency and Federal Bureau of Investigation are advising the Ukrainian government."

> Citing unnamed German security sources, Bild am Sonntag said the CIA and FBI agents were helping Kiev end the rebellion in the east of Ukraine and set up a functioning security structure.[3]

During the Cold War, Washington Supported Ukraine's Neo-Nazis

There is a longstanding relationship between U.S. intelligence and Nazi groups in Ukraine, which has a bearing on our understanding of recent events including the crimes committed by the Right Sector militia and National Guard in Odessa and Eastern Ukraine.

The *Organization of Ukrainian Nationalists* (OUN) (Організація Українських Націоналістів) led by Stepan Bandera, actively collaborated with Nazi Germany during World War II in the mass murder of Jews, Poles, Russians and Ukrainians under what was known as the *"Nachtigall Battalion"* (*Battalion Ukrainische Gruppe Nachtigall*, (Eng: the OUN Nightingale Battalion)

While news reports confirm U.S. support to the two neo-Nazi parties in the Petro Poroshenko regime, CIA support to Ukraine's OUN dates back to the Cold War era. Acknowledged by historians yet unknown to the American public was Washington's insidious *support of Ukraine's OUN neo-Nazis after World War II as a means of destabilizing the Soviet Union.*

This support was an integral part of what was called The Truman Doctrine formulated by State Department official George Kennan. (See Chapter I.)

In a bitter irony, following the defeat of Nazi Germany, the Truman administration instructed U.S. intelligence –at the height of the Cold War– to ensure the continuation of Nazi Germany's support to Ukraine's OUN *Nachtingall Battalion*, reshaped and transformed into a subversive guerrilla group under an Anglo-American acronym.

According to U.S. historian and former Under Secretary of the Air Force Townsend Hoopes and Rice University history professor Douglas Brinkely:

> When the Germans were driven out of the Ukraine, many OUN members who had served the Nazis' police formations and execution squads fled with them, but several thousand retreated into the Carpathian Mountains to fight another day against the hated Soviet government. It was this remaining Nightingale group that *fascinated the CIA and was recruited essentially en bloc. To bring its leaders to the United States for training and indoctrination* required special bureaucratic exertions, as well as an immigration law permitting the admission of one hundred such immigrants per year, provided *the Director of the CIA, the Attorney General, and the Commissioner of the Immigration and Naturalization Service all personally stated that the action was vital to national security.* As one army intelligence officer noted sardonically, one wing of the CIA was hunting Ukrainian Nazis to bring them to trial at Nuremberg, while another wing was recruiting them.
> *After training in the United States, the Nightingale leaders were parachuted into the Ukraine* to link up with their compatriots and to carry out measures of subversion, agitation, and sabotage, including assassination [against the Soviet Union].[4]

In the wake of World War II, the OUN led by Nazi collaborator Stepan Bandera was restructured. It was supported by a U.S. sponsored "Nightingale Operation" directed against the Soviet Union. Moreover, according to Stephen Dorril, *author of MI6: Inside the*

Covert World of Her Majesty's Secret Intelligence Service, the OUN was also endorsed by the British Secret Service MI6.

This complex historical background is important in assessing the contemporary relationship of U.S.-NATO to the two neo-Nazi parties Svoboda and Right Sector, both of which glorify the Nazi legacy of Stepan Bandera and the OUN.

There is continuity: What the historical record suggests is that U.S. intelligence from the "Truman Doctrine" to the Neocons (not to mention Obama) has supported Ukraine's Neo-Nazi entities. The latter constitute "intelligence assets" which are currently being deployed in the wake of the Cold war. The ultimate objective is to absorb Ukraine within the realm of NATO as well destabilize the Russian Federation.

Is U.S.-NATO Applying the "Syria Model" in Ukraine?

Of significance, Republican Senator John McCain will mingle with Al Qaeda leaders in Syria while also establishing a routine dialogue with the leader of the Neo-Nazi party Svoboda.

While the geopolitical context is different, there are certain obvious similarities. Innocent civilians are the victims of a U.S.-NATO military agenda which consists in supporting terrorist entities.

Ask John McCain. In both countries, the U.S. is in the pursuit of "real democracy" by supporting rather than combating terrorism.

Al Qaeda in Syria, neo-Nazis in Ukraine.

It's all part of "The New Normal".

Both the Al Nusra Front and the Right Sector have links to U.S. intelligence. In both Syria and Ukraine, Washington's intent is to destabilize and destroy the institutions of a sovereign country.

Killing civilians is a means to creating social divisiveness, thereby curtailing the development of a mass movement against U.S.-NATO.

What is at stake is a process of destabilization and *societal destruction*.

Al Nusrah is to Syria what Right Sector is to Ukraine. *They are the foot soldiers of the Western military alliance.*

While Al Nusrah is trained in Qatar and Saudi Arabia, Right Sector is trained in Poland. In both Ukraine and Syria, Western special forces are involved in overseeing terrorist operations.

In both Syria and Ukraine, the deaths of civilians are blamed on the victims.

The World is at a dangerous crossroads, East-West diplomacy is in crisis: The structures and composition of the Kiev proxy regime does not favor dialogue with the Russian government and military.

A scenario of military escalation leading to confrontation of Russia and NATO is a distinct possibility. Ukraine's National Security and National Defense Committee (RNBOU) which is controlled by neo-Nazis plays a central role in military affairs. In the confrontation with Moscow, decisions taken by the RNBOU headed by neo-Nazi Parubiy and his Brown Shirt deputy Dmytro Yarosh –in consultation with Washington and NATO headquarters in Brussels– could potentially have devastating consequences.

It goes without saying that "support" to the formation of a neo-Nazi government does not in any way imply the development of "fascist tendencies" within the White House, the State Department or the U.S. Congress.

"The flowering of democracy" in Ukraine –to use the words of the New York Times– is endorsed by Republicans and Democrats. It's a bipartisan project. Lest we forget, Senator John McCain is a firm supporter and friend of neo Nazi Svoboda leader Oleh Tyahnybok.

Notes

1. After Initial Triumph, Ukraine's Leaders Face Battle for Credibility, *New York Times*, March 1, 2014, emphasis added.
2. See Greg Rose, Ukraine Transition Government: Neo-Nazis in Control of Armed Forces, National Security, Economy, Justice and Education, Global Research, March 2, 2014.
3. Quoted by Agence France Presse, *Kiev Post*, May 4, 2014.
4. Air Force Townsend Hoopes and Brinkely, quoted in America Backed Ukraine Neo-Nazis In the Immediate Wake of World War II, Washington Blog, May 6, 2014.

Text written in March 2014. This chapter indicates the composition of the government at the very outset of the Kiev Coup regime which was installed with U.S.-NATO-EU support.

PART IV

BREAKING THE AMERICAN INQUISITION REVERSING THE TIDE OF WAR

CHAPTER XII

The "American Inquisition" and the "Global War on Terrorism"

Today's "Global War on Terrorism" (GWOT) is a modern form of inquisition. It has all the essential ingredients of the French and Spanish Inquisitions.

Going after "Islamic terrorists", carrying out a worldwide pre-emptive war to "Protect the American Homeland" are used to justify a military agenda.

"The Global War on Terrorism" (GWOT) is presented as a "Clash of Civilizations", a war between competing values and religions, when in reality it is an outright war of conquest, guided by strategic and economic objectives.

The GWOT is the ideological backbone of the American Empire. It defines U.S. military doctrine, including the pre-emptive use of nuclear weapons against the "state sponsors" of terrorism.

The pre-emptive "defensive war" doctrine and the "war on terrorism" against Al Qaeda constitute essential building blocks of America's National Security Strategy as formulated in early 2002. The objective is to present "pre-emptive military action" –meaning war as an act of "self-defense" against two categories of enemies, "rogue States" and "Islamic terrorists", both of which are said to possess weapons of mass destruction.

The logic of the "outside enemy" and the evildoer, allegedly responsible for American civilian deaths, prevails over common sense. In the inner consciousness of Americans, the attacks of September 11, 2001 justify acts of war and conquest:

> As was demonstrated by the losses on September 11, 2001, mass civilian casualties is the specific objective of terrorists and these losses would be exponentially more severe if terrorists acquired and used weapons of mass destruction.[1]

America's Inquisition

The legitimacy of the inquisition is not questioned. The "Global War on Terrorism" justifies a mammoth defense budget at the expense of health, education, and virtually every single category of (civilian) public expenditure.

The "Global War on Terrorism" requires "going after" the terrorists, using advanced weapons systems. It upholds a pre-emptive religious-like crusade against evil, which serves to obscure the real objectives of military action.

The lies underlying 9/11 are known and documented. The American people's acceptance of this crusade against evil is not based on any rational understanding or analysis of the facts.

America's inquisition is used to extend America's sphere of influence and justify military intervention, as part of an international campaign against "Islamic terrorists". Its ultimate objective, which is never mentioned in press reports, is territorial conquest and control over strategic resources.

The GWOT dogma is supported by an inquisitorial narrative enunciated and formulated by Washington's neoconservative think tanks and supported by the mainstream media. It is carried out by the military-intelligence establishment. It is embodied in presidential speeches and press conferences:

> We've been warned *there are evil people in this world*. We've been warned so vividly. … And we'll be alert. Your government is alert. The governors and mayors are alert that *evil folks still lurk out there*. As I said yesterday, people have declared war on America and they have made a terrible mistake. … My administration [George W. Bush] has a job to do and we're going to do it. *We will rid the world of the evil-doers*.[2]

An understanding of fundamental social and political events is replaced by a World of sheer fantasy, where "evil folks" are lurking.

The objective of the "Global War on Terrorism" launched in September 2001 has been to galvanize public support for a worldwide campaign against heresy. In the eyes of public opinion, possessing a "just cause" for waging war is central. A war is said to be Just if it is waged on moral, religious or ethical grounds. The mainstream media constitutes an instrument of war propaganda. It plays a central role in perpetuating the GWOT legend.

The Demonization of Muslims and the Battle for Oil

The U.S. led war in the broader Middle East Central Asian region consists in gaining control over extensive reserves of oil and natural gas. The Anglo-American oil giants also seek to gain control over oil and gas pipeline routes out of the region.

Muslim countries possess more than sixty percent of total oil reserves.[3] In contrast, the United States of America has barely two percent of total oil reserves. Iraq has five times more oil than the United States.

Demonization is applied to an enemy, which possesses more than sixty percent of the world's oil reserves. "Axis of evil", "rogue States", "failed nations", "Islamic terrorists": demonization and vilification are the ideological pillars of America's Inquisition. They serve as a casus belli for waging the Battle for Oil and Natural Gas.

> The Battle for Oil requires the demonization of those who possess the oil. The enemy is characterized as evil, with a view to justifying military action including the mass killing of civilians.[4]

The objective is to sustain the illusion that "America is under attack" by Al Qaeda. Under the American Inquisition, Washington has a self-proclaimed holy mandate to extirpate Islamic fundamentalism and "spread democracy" throughout the world.

"Going after the After Al Qaeda" or the Islamic State is part of a consensus. Fear and insecurity prevail over common sense. What we are dealing with is an outright and blind acceptance of the structures of power and political authority.

Historical Origins of The Inquisition

The American Inquisition as an ideological construct, is, in some regards, similar to the inquisitorial social order prevailing in France and Spain during The Middle Ages. The Inquisition, which started in France in the 12th century, was used as a justification for conquest and military intervention.

Initially it took the form of a campaign in southern France directed against the Cathars and Waldensians, which challenged the teachings of the Roman Catholic Church. The Cathar movement was a religious sect which was protected by the regional feudal order in southern France, against the dominion of the Catholic Church and the French monarchy in Paris. "The Cathars believed they were the true Christians and the Catholic Church was a false church, founded by the devil."

In the early thirteenth century, "Pope Innocent III declared a crusade against the Cathars" at the behest of the French royal family. The Crusade was in fact a war of conquest under the disguise of a campaign against heresy.

The Inquisition directed against heresy was intended to consolidate the Monarchy's territorial control. It provided a pretext to intervene militarily in south and southwestern France, using the authority of the Catholic Church as a façade.

The Inquisition became part of a political consensus, carried out by the Church's inquisitors, imposed and supported militarily by the ruling feudal order. Its purpose was to maintain and sustain the social and political order, extend the powers of the central State, subjugate regional powers in France, using the campaign against heresy as "a justification to wage war". Sounds familiar?

The Spanish Inquisition

In the fourteenth and fifteenth centuries, the Inquisition spread to other parts of Europe. In Italy, the inquisition went after nationalist movements in regions like Lombardy in the north, Venice and Sicily. It was used to suppress these political movements. In northern France and Germany, the inquisition used the pretext of small mystical sects, to intervene politically and militarily. Regional powers including local principalities refused to cooperate with the inquisition.

In today's world, this form of interventionism is carried out by sending in U.S. special forces to "help governments" to combat terrorism.

Spain, conquered by Muslims and in part reconquered by Christians in the 13th Century, was "religiously heterogeneous, and a tolerance had developed so Muslims, Christians, and Jews could live together in relative peace." Toward the end of the 15th Century, coinciding with a period of political and territorial consolidation, "Spanish tolerance changed abruptly. Spain saw the rise of a form of inquisition more ruthless and disruptive than anywhere else in Europe."[4]

The Spanish Inquisition was also characterized by a process of building a consensus, of going after the heretics and nonbelievers. The Inquisition was used to support the process of territorial consolidation in the Iberian peninsula. The objective was to reinforce the absolute monarchy and the powers of the landed aristocracy against the Muslim and Jewish merchant classes.

The Spanish Inquisition was executed at the behest of Queen Isabel, Reina Catolica. In 1483, The Reyes Catolicos, Isabel de Castilla and Ferdinando de Aragon, established a Council to direct the Inquisition. Tomas de Torquemada, an advisor to Isabel become the first General Inquisitor. Torquemado had previously preached against the Jewish and Muslim Converts (Conversos). The objective was to repress the upcoming merchant classes. *"One country, one ruler, one faith"* became the mandate of the General Inquisitor.

The pope upheld the inquisition; the hidden agenda was the feudal order and the Spanish led colonial wars. The Spanish inquisition lasted for three hundred years.

Today in America, the General inquisitor is the Secretary of the Department of Homeland Security.

The Legal Apparatus

The inquisition in the Middle Ages would collect accusations:

> If two witnesses under oath accused someone of heresy, the accused person would be summoned to appear. Opinions, prejudices, rumors, and gossip were all accepted as evidence. The accused was never told the names of the accusers, nor even the exact charges.
>
> Inquisitors examined the accused in secret. Anyone who refused to confess immediately was assumed to be guilty. Inquisitors were trained only in religion, and they would try to trap the accused with religious questions. For example, an inquisitor might ask, "Do you believe what the holy church believes?"

> "I am a faithful Christian," the fearful suspect might reply. "So!" the inquisitor might shout. "We already know you believe in heresies! You're saying your beliefs are the true Christianity and the church is false![5]

No lawyers were allowed, because it was considered heresy to defend a heretic:

> They would torture those who refused to recant. During torture, the religious inquisitors would stand by as witnesses to record confessions or take down the names of other heretics. The government also carried out the final sentence of imprisonment or death.
>
> Those who recanted immediately might receive a fairly light sentence – saying prayers, fasting, being whipped in public, or making a pilgrimage. Some who recanted were forced to wear a yellow cross of felt sewn on all their clothing. The cross marked them as a former heretic, and many people would stay away from them in fear.
>
> Many who refused to recant right away were sentenced to prison for life. If they refused to recant at all, the Inquisition turned them over to government authorities to be burned alive. Some inquisitors were so thorough that they went after the dead. If a dead person had been accused of heresy (while still living), his or her bones could be dug up and burned.
>
> For most accused heretics, there was no appeal. A few rich or powerful people might beg the pope to change a sentence, but for most of the condemned, the sentence was final. The families of those sent to prison or to the stake lost their property.[6]

Today's Inquisitorial Order

Today's legal system in America has all the essential features of an inquisitorial order. Torture is permitted "under certain circumstances", according to an August 2002 Justice Department "legal opinion":

> If a government employee were to torture a suspect in captivity, "he would be doing so in order to prevent further attacks on the United States by the Al Qaeda terrorist

network," said the memo, from the Justice Department's office of legal counsel, written in response to a CIA request for legal guidance. It added that arguments centering on "necessity and self-defense could provide justifications that would eliminate any criminal liability" later.[7]

"Interrogation methods" bordering on torture do not imply a unconstitutional infringement according to the U.S. Justice Department:

> Even if an interrogation method might arguably cross the line drawn in Section and application of the stature was not held to be an unconstitutional infringement of the President's Commander in Chief authority, we believe that under current circumstances [the war on terrorism] certain justification defenses might be available that would potentially eliminate criminal liability.[8]

Anybody who doubts the legitimacy of the American inquisition (i.e. 9/11 and the "Global War on Terrorism") is a heretic conspiracy theorist or an accomplice of the terrorists.

The American Inquisition is part of a Bipartisan Consensus. Both the Democrats and the Republicans support the American Inquisition. It is also supported by several prominent "progressive" intellectuals. (See Chapter XIII).

Since September 2001, "Going after Osama bin Laden" has been part of the election platform of both political parties:

> I [Barack Obama] argued for *more resources and more troops to finish the fight against the terrorists who actually attacked us on 9/11*, and made clear that *we must take out Osama bin Laden* and his lieutenants if we have them in our sights[9]

> We [John McCain during the 2008 election campaign] *have dealt a serious blow to al Qaeda in recent years. But they are not defeated, and they'll strike us again* if they can.[10]

There is an "outside enemy". The Homeland is under attack. Islamic terrorists "threaten our way of life". "We must defend ourselves" pre-emptively against Al Qaeda and the Islamic State.

U.S. Northern Command (NORTHCOM), with headquarters at the Petersen Air Force base in Colorado was established in early 2002 to protect America against a terrorist attack. It was presented to public opinion as a response to the 9/11 attacks. The real strategic objectives of Northern Command using sophisticated "aero defense weapons" including nuclear warheads, are not mentioned. Are nukes to be used against Al Qaeda?

Political Consensus

The mouthpiece of America's inquisitorial order is the Western corporate media.

People who question the validity of any of these statements or who have doubts about who is behind the 9/11 attacks, are considered to be accomplices of those who threaten the American Homeland.

In 1232, Pope Gregory IX set up a system of special religious courts called The Inquisition. The Dominican friars were sent out to find and question heretics:

> *Heresy cannot be destroyed unless heretics are destroyed* and ... their defenders and [supporters] are destroyed, and this is effected in two ways: ... they are converted to the true catholic faith, or ... burned.[11]

Those who refused to recant, which means give up their heresy, were burned alive.

Today's Patriot Act, the military courts, the Guantanamo concentration camp, the CIA rendition camps, Abu Ghraib, etc. are part of an advanced inquisitorial system. Terrorist suspects are held incommunicado. They are tortured, tried by military courts and sentenced. They are not given the right to recant.

The objective is not to "make the world safer" by putting the terrorists behind bars. The show trials of the alleged terrorists perform an important social function. They are an integral part of the Pentagon's disinformation campaign. Quite concretely, they give a real face to a fictitious outside enemy. They sustain the illusion, in the inner consciousness of Americans, that the "Islamic terrorists" constitute a real threat.

The arrests, trials and sentences of "Islamic terrorists" sustain the legitimacy of America's Homeland Security State and its inquisitorial legal and law enforcement apparatus.

The ultimate objective is to instill in the minds of millions of Americans that the enemy is real and the U.S. Administration will protect the lives of its citizens.

America's Inquisition does Not Persecute "Liberals" and "Antiwar Activists"

Washington does not silence its antiwar critics. Quite the opposite. The inquisitorial social order allows certain forms of dissent. It is politically correct under a "democracy" to condemn U.S. foreign policy in the strongest terms.

What is not allowed is to question the inquisition.

Those who oppose the U.S. Administration are not branded as heretics. Many "Progressives", Liberals and antiwar activists, led by prominent intellectuals, firmly believe that Muslims were behind the 9/11 attacks. "*We are against the war, but we support the war on terrorism.*"

The New World Order builds a political and media consensus (that is, the GWOT) but at the same time it creates and molds its own opposition. It establishes the limits of dissent. It "manufactures dissent". (See Chapter XII.)

The presidential candidates in the bipartisan race are supported by powerful corporate interests including the oil companies, Wall Street and the defense contractors.

At the same time, these same corporate interests, through their various foundations (including Ford, Rockefeller, Gates, et al), support and finance a number of Liberal/Progressive organizations and alternative media.

9/11 is the cornerstone of the American Inquisition.

The lies underlying 9/11 are accepted by the mainstream antiwar movement.

U.S. foreign policy is condemned, but the "Global War on Terrorism" is upheld. Wittingly or unwittingly, this endorsement of the GWOT by those who claim to be opposed to the U.S. administration, provides a legitimacy to the inquisitorial order, which underlies the actual practice of U.S. foreign policy.

On the other hand, those who have serious doubts regarding the official 9/11 narrative, including the 9/11 Truth Movement, are branded as heretics and nonbelievers.

Torture

> The Spanish Inquisition was particularly terrifying because of its inherent characteristics. The accused never knew who their accusers were. Once arrested, the accused heretic's properties were seized....
>
> These properties were then administered at first by the Crown, and later by the General Inquisitor....
>
> Even if the accused was now a devout Christian, he was tried as severely as possible because of his roots. The accused was also not allowed to have a lawyer or counsel for his defense, and the names of all witnesses were kept secret from him.[12]

Torture was the order of the day. The accused were not allowed to have a lawyer.

The torture methods applied by today's CIA inquisitors bear a canny resemblance to the torture techniques used by the Inquisitors in the Middle Ages, including the water torment or *aselli*, commonly referred to in CIA jargon as "water boarding":

> Because the trials were for spiritual matters, the Church handled them. However, the punishments were usually very much physical, so they were handled by the state. There were many means of this physical torture for confession. The two most famous or infamous were the *strappado* or pulley, and the *aselli* or water torment.[13]

Alfred McCoy reports in the regard that the CIA:

> had often added to their no-touch repertoire *physical methods reminiscent of the Inquisition's trademark tortures – strappado, question de l'eau, "crippling stork," and "masks of mockery."* At the CIA's center near Kabul in 2002, for instance, American interrogators forced prisoners "to stand with their hands chained to the ceiling and their feet shackled," an effect similar to the strappado. In-

stead of the Inquisition's iron-framed "crippling stork" to contort the victim's body, CIA interrogators made their victims assume similar "stress positions" without any external mechanism, aiming again for the psychological effect of self-induced pain.[14]

In Spain, in the sixteenth century, the inquisition was accepted. It was a consensus. The population was led to believe that it was a good thing and that torture "served to purify society".

A bishop came out and shouted out the names of the condemned. then the heretics were led out, wearing black robes decorated with red demons and flames. officials of the government tied them to the stake.
Do you give up your heresy against the holy church?" a priest would challenge.
Anyone who repented would be strangled to death before the fires were lit. most, however, stood silent or defiant. the fires were lit, and the square echoed with the screams of the heretics and cheers from the crowd.[15]

Anybody who dared to question the validity of this "war on terrorism" was himself branded a terrorist and subjected to the anti-terrorist laws, which at the time, in Spain, was death.

In today's inquisitorial environment, most people are skeptical regarding the official 9/11 narrative, but nobody dares question the validity of the "War on Terrorism".

"These are bad people, and we must go after them, take them out." While the wording is different, the ideological thrust bears a canny resemblance to the Spanish Inquisition.

The ultimate objective is to subdue the citizens, totally depoliticize social life in America, prevent people from thinking and conceptualizing, from analyzing facts and challenging the legitimacy of the inquisitorial social order which rules America.

The Big Lie becomes the Truth. Realities are turned upside down. War becomes peace, a worthwhile "humanitarian undertaking", Peaceful dissent becomes heresy.

The objective is to create an atmosphere of fear and insecurity, with a view to upholding the New World Order.

In the words of Monty Python:

> NOBODY expects the Spanish Inquisition!
> Our chief weapon is surprise...surprise and fear...fear and surprise....
> Our two weapons are fear and surprise...and ruthless efficiency....
> Our *three* weapons are fear, surprise, and ruthless efficiency...and an almost fanatical devotion to the Pope....
> Our *four*...no... *Amongst* our weapons.... Amongst our weaponry... are such elements as fear, surprise....
> I'll come in again.[16]

Notes

1. National Security Strategy, White House, Washington, 2002.
2. George W. Bush, CNN, September 16, 2001, emphasis added.
3. Michel Chossudovsky, The "Demonization" of Muslims and the Battle for Oil, Global Research, January 4, 2007.
4. See Michel Chossudovsky, 9/11 and the "American Inquisition", Global Research, September 11, 2008. See also Bill of Rights in Action at http://www.crf-usa.org/bill-of-rights-in-action/.
5. *Ibid*.
6. Bill of Rights in Action, http://www.crf-usa.org/bill-of-rights-in-action/ See also History of the Inquisition.
7. See *Washington Post*, June 7, 2004.
8. Complete August 2, 2002 Justice Department Memorandum in pdf at http://www.washingtonpost.com/wp-srv/nation/documents/dojinterrogation-memo20020801.pdf.
9. Barack Obama, Acceptance Speech, National Democratic Convention, Denver, August 2008.
10. John McCain, Acceptance Speech, Republican National Convention, St Paul, September 2008.
11. Henry Charles Lea, A History of the Inquisition of the Middle Ages, p. 535, 1887, emphasis added.
12. Jason L. Slade, The Spanish Inquisition, August 6, 1996.
13. *Ibid.*
14. Alfred McCoy, The Hidden History of CIA Torture: America's Road to Abu Ghraib, Global Research, December 2004, emphasis added.
15. Quoted in Bill of Rights in Action, *op cit.*
16. Monthy Python, The Spanish Inquisition, BBC quoted by Wikipedia

An earlier version of this text was first published in September 2008.

Chapter XIII

"Manufactured Dissent", Colored Revolutions and the Antiwar Movement in Crisis

The antiwar movement in several Western countries is in crisis, dominated by self-proclaimed "progressives". While America's war on Iraq was condemned outright, the wars on Yugoslavia, Afghanistan, Libya and Syria were heralded as "just wars" or "humanitarian interventions". A significant segment of the U.S. antiwar movement condemns the war but endorses the campaign against international terrorism, which constitutes the backbone of U.S. military doctrine. (See Chapter XI)

Historically, many progressive social movements have been infiltrated, their leaders co-opted and manipulated, through the corporate funding of non-governmental organizations, trade unions and political parties. The ultimate purpose of "funding dissent" is to prevent the protest movement from challenging the legitimacy of the dominant economic elites including Wall Street, Big Oil, the Military Industrial complex, the Bio-tech conglomerates and the corporate media.

A large segment of "progressive" opinion in the U.S. and Western Europe is tacitly supportive of NATO's *Responsiblity to Protect (R2P)* "humanitarian" mandate to the extent that these war plans are being carried out with the "rubber stamp" of civil society. Prominent "progressive" authors as well independent media outlets were supportive of regime change and NATO's sponsored humanitarian intervention in Libya. Similarly, many "progressives" have rallied in support of the U.S.-NATO sponsored "opposition" in Syria.

Let us be under no illusions: This pseudo-progressive discourse is an instrument of propaganda. Several prominent "left" intellectuals –who claim to be opposed to U.S. imperialism– have supported the imposition of "no fly zones" and "humanitarian interventions" against sovereign countries.

"Progressives" are funded and co-opted by elite foundations including Ford, Rockefeller, et al. The corporate elites have sought to fragment the people's movement into a vast "do it yourself" mosaic. War and globalization are no longer in the forefront of civil society activism. "Activism" tends to be piecemeal. There is no integrated anti-globalization anti-war movement. The relationship between the economic and social crisis and America's global military agenda is not addressed:

> *Everything the [Ford] Foundation did could be regarded as "making the World safe for capitalism", reducing social tensions by helping to comfort the afflicted, provide safety valves for the angry, and improve the functioning of government.*[1] (McGeorge Bundy, National Security Advisor to presidents John F. Kennedy and Lyndon Johnson (1961-1966), President of the Ford Foundation (1966-1979))

> By providing the funding and the policy framework to many concerned and dedicated people working within the non-profit sector, the ruling class is able to co-opt leadership from grassroots communities, ... and is able to make the funding, accounting, and evaluation components of the work so time consuming and onerous that social justice work is virtually impossible under these conditions.[2]

"Manufactured Consent" versus "Manufactured Dissent"

The term "manufactured consent" was initially coined by Edward S. Herman and Noam Chomsky. "Manufacturing consent" describes a propaganda model used by the corporate media to sway public opinion and "inculcate individuals with values and beliefs...":

> The mass media serve as a system for communicating messages and symbols to the general populace. It is their function to amuse, entertain, and inform, and to inculcate individuals with the values, beliefs, and codes of behavior that will integrate them into the institutional structures of the larger society. In a world of concentrated wealth and major conflicts of class interest, to fulfill this role requires systematic propaganda.[3]

"Manufacturing consent" implies manipulating and shaping public opinion. It establishes conformity and acceptance to authority and social hierarchy. It seeks compliance to an established social order. "Manufacturing consent" describes the submission of public opinion to the mainstream media narrative, to its lies and fabrications.

In this chapter we focus on a related concept, namely the subtle process of "manufacturing dissent" (rather than "consent"), which plays a decisive role in serving the interests of the corporate elites.

Under contemporary capitalism, the illusion of democracy must prevail. It is in the interest of the corporate elites to accept dissent and protest as a feature of the system inasmuch as they do not threaten the established social order. The purpose is not to repress dissent, but, on the contrary, to shape and mould the protest movement, to set the outer limits of dissent, to control dissent.

To maintain their legitimacy, the economic elites favor limited and controlled forms of opposition, with a view to preventing the development of radical forms of protest, which might shake the very foundations and institutions of global capitalism. In other words, "manufacturing dissent" acts as a "safety valve", which protects and sustains the New World Order.

To be effective, however, the process of "manufacturing dissent" must be carefully regulated and monitored by those who are the object of the protest movement.

"Funding Dissent"

How is the process of manufacturing dissent achieved?

Essentially by "funding dissent", namely by channeling financial resources from those who are the object of the protest movement to those who are involved in organizing the protest movement.

Co-optation is not limited to buying the favors of politicians. The economic elites –which control major foundations– also oversee the funding of numerous NGOs and civil society organizations, which historically have been involved in the protest movement against the established economic and social order. The programs of many NGOs, antiwar collectives and people's movements rely heavily on funding from both public as well as private foundations including the Ford, Rockefeller, McCarthy foundations, among others.

The anti-globalization movement is opposed to Wall Street and the Texas oil giants controlled by Rockefeller, et al. Yet the foundations and charities of Rockefeller et al will generously fund "progressive" anti-capitalist networks as well as environmentalists (opposed to Big Oil) with a view to ultimately overseeing and shaping their various activities.

The mechanisms of "manufacturing dissent" require a manipulative environment, a process of arm-twisting and subtle co-optation of individuals within progressive organizations, including anti-war coalitions, environmentalists and the anti-globalization movement.

Whereas the mainstream media "manufactures consent", the complex network of NGOs (including segments of the alternative media) are used by the corporate elites to mold and manipulate the protest movement.

Following the deregulation of the global financial system in the 1990s and the rapid enrichment of the financial establishment, funding through foundations and charities has skyrocketed.

In a bitter irony, part of the fraudulent financial gains on Wall Street in recent years have been recycled to the elites' corporate tax exempt foundations and charities. These windfall financial gains have not only been used to buy out politicians, they have also been channeled to NGOs, research institutes, community centers, church groups, environmentalists, alternative media, human rights groups, etc. "Manufactured dissent" also applies to the "corporate left" and "progressive" media, funded by NGOs or directly by the foundations.

The inner objective is to "manufacture dissent" and establish the boundaries of a "politically correct" opposition. In turn, many NGOs are infiltrated by informants often acting on behalf of western intelligence agencies. Moreover, an increasingly large segment of the progressive alternative news media on the internet has become dependent on funding from corporate foundations and charities.

Piecemeal Activism

Dissent has been compartmentalized. Separate "issue oriented" protest movements (for example, environment, anti-globalization, peace, women's rights, climate change) are encouraged and generously funded as opposed to a cohesive mass movement. This mosaic was already prevalent in the counter G7 summits and People's Summits of the 1990s.

History of the Anti-Globalization Movement

The Seattle 1999 counter-summit is invariably upheld as a triumph for the anti-globalization movement: "a historic coalition of activists shut down the World Trade Organization (WTO) Summit in Seattle, the spark that ignited a global anti-corporate movement."[4]

Seattle was an indeed an important landmark in the history of the mass movement. Over 50,000 people from diverse backgrounds, civil society organizations, human rights, labor unions, environmentalists had come together in a common pursuit. Their goal was to forcefully dismantle the neoliberal agenda including its institutional base.

But Seattle also marked a major reversal. With mounting dissent from all sectors of society, the official WTO Summit desperately needed the token participation of civil society leaders "on the inside", to give the appearance of being "democratic" "on the outside".

While thousands of people had converged on Seattle, what occurred behind the scenes was a de facto victory for neoliberalism. A handful of civil society organizations, formally opposed to the WTO had contributed to legitimizing the WTO's global trading architecture. Instead of challenging the WTO as an an illegal intergovernmental body, they agreed to a pre-summit dialogue with the WTO and Western governments."Accredited NGO participants were invited to mingle in a friendly environment with ambassadors, trade ministers and Wall Street tycoons at several of the official events including the numerous cocktail parties and receptions."[5]

> Under the New World Order, the ritual of inviting "civil society" leaders into the inner circles of power –while simultaneously repressing the rank and file– serves several important functions. First, it says to the World that the critics of globalization "must make concessions" to earn the right to mingle. Second, it conveys the illusion that while the global elites should –under what is euphemistically called democracy– be subject to criticism, they nonetheless rule legitimately. And third, it says "there is no alternative"

to globalization: fundamental change is not possible and the most we can hope is to engage with these rulers in an ineffective "give and take".

While the "Globalizers" may adopt a few progressive phrases to demonstrate they have good intentions, their fundamental goals are not challenged. And what this "civil society mingling" does is to reinforce the clutch of the corporate establishment while weakening and dividing the protest movement. An understanding of this process of co-optation is important, because tens of thousands of the most principled young people in Seattle, Prague and Quebec City [1999-2001] were involved in the anti-globalization protests because they reject the notion that money is everything, because they reject the impoverishment of millions and the destruction of fragile Earth so that a few may get richer.

This rank and file and some of their leaders as well, are to be applauded. But we need to go further. We need to challenge the right of the "Globalizers" to rule. This requires that we rethink the strategy of protest. Can we move to a higher plane, by launching mass movements in our respective countries, movements that bring the message of what Globalization is doing, to ordinary people? For they are the force that must be mobilized to challenge those who plunder the Globe.[6]

The hidden agenda was to weaken and divide the protest movement and orient the anti-globalization movement into areas that would not directly threaten the interests of the business establishment.

Funded by private foundations (including Ford, Rockefeller, Rockefeller Brothers, Charles Stewart Mott, The Foundation for Deep Ecology), these "accredited" civil society organizations had positioned themselves as lobby groups, acting formally on behalf of the people's movement. Led by prominent and committed activists, their hands were tied. They ultimately contributed (unwittingly) to weakening the anti-globalization movement by accepting the legitimacy of what was essentially an illegal organization. The 1994 Marrakech Summit agreement which led to

the creation of the WTO [World Trade Organization] on
January 1, 1995 was never questioned.[7]

The NGO leaders were fully aware as to where the money was coming from. Yet within the U.S. and European NGO community, the
foundations and charities are considered to be independent philan-
thropic bodies, separate from the corporations; namely the Rockefeller
Brothers Foundation, for instance, is considered to be separate and distinct from the Rockefeller family empire of banks and oil companies.

With salaries and operating expenses depending on private foundations, it became an accepted routine: In a twisted logic, *the battle
against corporate capitalism was being fought using the funds from
the tax exempt foundations owned by corporate capitalism.* An absurd proposition.

The NGOs were caught in a straightjacket; their very existence
depended on continued funding from the foundations. Their activities were closely monitored. The very nature of anti-capitalist activism was indirectly controlled by the capitalists through their tax
free foundations.

*Global capitalism finances anti-capitalism: an absurd and con-
tradictory relationship.* "Another World is Possible", but it cannot be
meaningfully achieved under the present arrangement. A shake-up of
the World Social Forum, of its organizational structure, its funding
arrangements and leadership is required.

*There can be no meaningful mass movement when dissent is gen-
erously funded by those same corporate interests which are the target of the protest movement.*

The "Revolution Business"

The imperial World Order creates its own opposition.

"Color Revolutions" financed by Wall Street unfold in different
countries (for example, Egypt, Ukraine, Georgia, Thailand). The CIA
through various front organizations has infiltrated mass movements
in different parts of the World.

The Occupy Movement in the U.S. is infiltrated and manipulated.

The Centre for Applied Non-Violent Action and Strategies
(CANVAS), for instance, under the auspices of Serbia's OTPOR is
a CIA sponsored entity which describes itself as "an International

network of trainers and consultants" involved in the "Revolution Business".

Funded by the National Endowment for Democracy (NED), it constitutes a consulting outfit, advising and training U.S. sponsored opposition groups in more than forty countries. Its clenched-fist logo has been adopted by numerous "revolutionary" groups.

In turn, a panoply of alternative media upholds the "Color Revolutions" as constituting a "Great Awakening", a mass movement directed against the very foundations of the capitalist World order.

In Egypt, for instance, several organizations involved in the Arab Spring in 2011 including Kifaya and the April 6 Student Movement were directly supported by U.S. foundations and the U.S. embassy in Cairo. In a bitter irony, Washington was supporting the Mubarak dictatorship, including its atrocities, while also backing and financing its detractors, through the activities of Freedom House (FH) and the National Endowment for Democracy (NED). Both of these foundations have links to the U.S. State Department and the U.S. Congress.

Under the auspices of Freedom House, Egyptian dissidents and opponents of Hosni Mubarak had been received in May 2008 by Condoleezza Rice at the State Department and the U.S. Congress. The Egyptian pro-democracy delegation to the State Department was described by Condoleezza Rice as "The Hope for the Future of Egypt". In May 2009, Hillary Clinton met a delegation of Egyptian dissidents, several of which had met Condoleezza Rice a year earlier.

9/11 Truth and America's Wars

In recent history, with the exception of Iraq, the so-called Western Left namely "Progressives" have paid lip service to U.S.-NATO military interventions in Yugoslavia, Afghanistan, Libya and Syria. "Progressives" also support the official 9/11 version of events. They deny 9/11 Truth.

"Progressives" acknowledge that the U.S. was under attack on 9/11 and that the war on Afghanistan was a "Just War". In the case of Afghanistan, the "self-defense" argument was accepted at face value as a legitimate response to the 9/11 attacks, without examining the fact that the U.S. administration had not only supported the

"Islamic terror network", it was also instrumental in the installation of the Taliban government in 1995-96.

In 2001, when Afghanistan was bombed and later invaded, "progressives" largely upheld the administration's "just cause" military doctrine. In the wake of 9/11, the antiwar movement against the illegal invasion of Afghanistan was isolated. The trade unions and civil society organizations had swallowed the media's lies and government propaganda. They had accepted a war of retribution against the people of Afghanistan. Several prominent "left-leaning" intellectuals upheld the "war on terrorism" agenda.

Media disinformation prevailed. People were misled as to the nature and objectives underlying the invasion of Afghanistan. Osama bin Laden and the Taliban were identified as the prime suspects of the 9/11 attacks, without a shred of evidence and without addressing the historical relationship between Al Qaeda and the U.S. intelligence apparatus.

In this regard, understanding 9/11 is crucial in formulating a consistent antiwar position. 9/11 is the pillar of U.S. war propaganda; it sustains the illusion of an outside enemy, it justifies pre-emptive military intervention.

The logic pertaining to Syria was somewhat different. From the outset of the war in 2011, "progressives" and mainstream "antiwar" organizations supported so-called Syria opposition forces without acknowledging that the mainstay of these forces was composed of Al Qaeda affiliated terrorists, recruited, trained and financed by U.S.-NATO and their allies including Israel, Turkey, Qatar and Saudi Arabia.

These antiwar groups, which previously supported NATO's intervention in Libya in 2011, have casually blamed the Syrian government for the atrocities committed by the U.S. sponsored Al Qaeda rebels.

Rebuilding the Antiwar Movement

What is required is to rebuild a mass movement. And this cannot be led by organizations which are financed by corporate foundations.[8]

The social base as well as the organizational structure of the antiwar movement must be transformed. America's "Long War" is an

imperialist project which sustains the financial structures and institutional foundations of the capitalist World Order. Behind this military agenda are powerful corporate interests including an extensive
propaganda apparatus.

War and the Economic Crisis are intimately related. The worldwide imposition of neoliberal macro-economic policy measures is
part of the broader imperial agenda. War is also an instrument of
economic conquest. And consequently, the broader movement
against neoliberalism must be integrated into the antiwar movement.

Breaking the "Big Lie" which presents war as a humanitarian undertaking, means breaking a criminal project of global destruction,
in which the quest for profit is the overriding force.

The holding of mass demonstrations and antiwar protests is not
enough. What is required is the development of a broad and well-organized grassroots antiwar network, nationally and internationally,
which challenges the structures of power and authority as well as
the nature of the capitalist World order. People must mobilize not
only against the military agenda, the authority of the state and its officials must also be challenged.

The mainstream media must be targeted. The lies and fabrications
which sustain the war agenda must be uncovered. A meaningful antiwar movement requires breaking the "war on terrorism" consensus
and its propaganda apparatus.

Breaking the lies behind the official 9/11 narrative is absolutely essential because without the 9/11 narrative, the legitimacy of the "global
war on terrorism" collapses like a deck of cards. Without the 9/11 legend, the warmongers in high office do not have a leg to stand on.

There are no easy solutions. A major upheaval in power structures
within society is required.

To reverse the tide of war and globalization requires a massive
campaign of networking and outreach to inform people across the
land, nationally and internationally, in neighborhoods, workplaces,
parishes, schools, universities and municipalities, on the nature of
the imperial project, its military and economic dimensions, not to
mention the dangers of a U.S. sponsored nuclear war. This movement must also occur within the Armed Forces (including NATO)
with a view to challenging the legitimacy of the military agenda.

Notes

1. McGeorge Bundy, National Security Advisor to Presidents John F. Kennedy and Lyndon Johnson (1961-1966), President of the Ford Foundation, (1966-1979).

2. Paul Kivel, *You Call this Democracy, Who Benefits, Who Pays and Who Really Decides*, 2004, p. 122.

3. Edward S. Herman and Noam Chomsky, *Manufacturing Consent*, Anthem Books, 1988.

4. See Naomi Klein, Copenhagen: Seattle Grows Up, The Nation, November 13, 2009.

5. Michel Chossudovsky, Seattle and Beyond: Disarming the New World Order, *Covert Action Quarterly*, November 1999.

6. Michel Chossudovsky, The Quebec Wall, April 2001

7. *Ibid*.

8. For a detailed analysis on Reversing the Tide of War, see Michel Chossudovsky, *Towards a World War III Scenario: The Dangers of Nuclear War*, Global Research, Montreal, 2011, 2012, Chapter XI.

An earlier version of this chapter was written in 2008.

INDEX

GLOBAL RESEARCH PUBLISHERS

Towards a World War III Scenario: The Dangers of Nuclear War
MICHEL CHOSSUDOVSKY
ISBN 978-0-9737147-5-3 (2012), 102 pages.

The U.S. has embarked on a military adventure, "a long war", which threatens the future of humanity. U.S.-NATO weapons of mass destruction are portrayed as instruments of peace. Mini-nukes are said to be "harmless to the surrounding civilian population". Pre-emptive nuclear war is portrayed as a "humanitarian undertaking".

While one can conceptualize the loss of life and destruction resulting from present-day wars including Iraq and Afghanistan, it is impossible to fully comprehend the devastation which might result from a Third World War, using "new technologies" and advanced weapons, until it occurs and becomes a reality. The international community has endorsed nuclear war in the name of world peace. "Making the world safer" is the justification for launching a military operation which could potentially result in a nuclear holocaust.

The object of this book is to forcefully reverse the tide of war, challenge the war criminals in high office and the powerful corporate lobby groups which support them.

Award winning author and economics professor Michel Chossudovsky is Director of the Centre for Research on Globalization (CRG).

The Global Economic Crisis:
The Great Depression of the XXI Century
MICHEL CHOSSUDOVSKY AND ANDREW GAVIN
MARSHALL, EDITORS
ISBN 978-0973714739 (2010), 416 pages

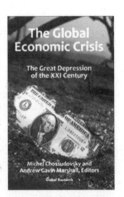

In all major regions of the world, the economic recession is deep-seated, resulting in mass unemployment, the collapse of state social programs and the impoverishment of millions of people. The meltdown of financial markets was the result of institutionalized fraud and financial manipulation. The economic crisis is accompanied by a worldwide process of militarization, a "war without borders" led by the U.S. and its NATO allies.

This book takes the reader through the corridors of the Federal Reserve, into the plush corporate boardrooms on Wall Street where far-reaching financial transactions are routinely undertaken.

Each of the authors in this timely collection digs beneath the gilded surface to reveal a complex web of deceit and media distortion which serves to conceal the workings of the global economic system and its devastating impacts on people's lives.

Seeds of Destruction:
The Hidden Agenda of Genetic Manipulation
F. WILLIAM ENGDAHL
ISBN 978-0-937147-2-2 (2007), 341 pages

This skillfully researched book focuses on how a small socio-political American elite seeks to establish control over the very basis of human survival: the provision of our daily bread. "*Control the food and you control the people.*"

This is no ordinary book about the perils of GMO. Engdahl takes the reader inside the corridors of power, into the backrooms of the science labs, behind closed doors in the corporate boardrooms.

The author cogently reveals a diabolical world of profit-driven political intrigue and government corruption and coercion, where genetic manipulation and the patenting of life forms are used to gain worldwide control over food production. If the book often reads as a crime story, that should come as no surprise. For that is what it is.

Engdahl's carefully argued critique goes far beyond the familiar controversies surrounding the practice of genetic modification as a scientific technique. The book is an eye-opener, a must-read for all those committed to the causes of social justice and world peace.

F. William Engdahl is a leading analyst of the New World Order and author of the best-selling book on oil and geopolitics, A Century of War: Anglo-American Politics and the New World Order.

America's "War on Terrorism"
MICHEL CHOSSUDOVSKY
ISBN 0-9737147-1-9 (2005), 387 pages

In this 2005 best-selling title, the author blows away the smokescreen put up by the mainstream media that 9/11 was an attack on America by "Islamic terrorists". Through meticulous research, the author uncovers a military-intelligence ploy behind the September 11 attacks, and the cover-up and complicity of key members of the Bush administration.

This expanded edition, which includes twelve new chapters, focuses on the use of 9/11 as a pretext for the invasion and illegal occupation of Iraq, the militarization of justice and law enforcement and the repeal of democracy.

According to Chossudovsky, the "war on terrorism" is a complete fabrication based on the illusion that one man, Osama bin Laden, outwitted the $40 billion-a-year American intelligence apparatus. The "war on terrorism" is a war of conquest. Globalization is the final march to the New World Order, dominated by Wall Street and the U.S. military-industrial complex.

September 11, 2001 provides a justification for waging a war without borders. Washington's agenda consists in extending the frontiers of the American empire to facilitate complete U.S. corporate control, while installing within America the institutions of the Homeland Security State. Chossudovsky peels back layers of rhetoric to reveal a complex web of deceit aimed at luring the American people and the rest of the world into accepting a military solution which threatens the future of humanity.

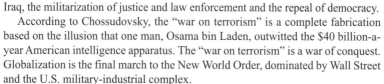

***The Globalization of Poverty
and the New World Order***

MICHEL CHOSSUDOVSKY

ISBN 09737147-0-0 (2003), 403 pages

In this new and expanded edition of Chossudovsky's international best-seller, the author outlines the contours of a New World Order which feeds on human poverty and the destruction of the environment, generates social apartheid, encourages racism and ethnic strife and undermines the rights of women. The result as his detailed examples from all parts of the world show so convincingly, is a globalization of poverty.

This book is a skillful combination of lucid explanation and cogently argued critique of the fundamental directions in which our world is moving financially and economically.

In this new enlarged edition – which includes ten new chapters and a new introduction – the author reviews the causes and consequences of famine in Sub-Saharan Africa, the dramatic meltdown of financial markets, the demise of state social programs and the devastation resulting from corporate downsizing and trade liberalization.